REEDS
OCEAN
HANDBOOK

BILL JOHNSON

Thomas Reed
An imprint of Bloomsbury Publishing Plc

50 Bedford Square
London
WC1B 3DP
UK

1385 Broadway
New York
NY 10018
USA

www.bloomsbury.com

REEDS, ADLARD COLES NAUTICAL and the Buoy logo are trademarks of
Bloomsbury Publishing Plc

First published 2015

© Bill Johnson, 2015

British Library Cataloguing-in-Publication Data
A catalogue record for this book is available from the British Library.

Library of Congress Cataloguing-in-Publication data has been applied for.

ISBN: PB: 978-1-4729-1306-7
ePDF: 978-1-4729-2143-7
ePub: 978-1-4729-2142-0

2 4 6 8 10 9 7 5 3 1

Typeset in 9 on 11 pt Myriad Light by Margaret Brain
Printed and bound in China by Toppan Leefung Printing

Bloomsbury Publishing Plc makes every effort to ensure that the papers used in
the manufacture of our books are natural, recyclable products made from wood
grown in well-managed forests. Our manufacturing processes conform to the
environmental regulations of the country of origin.

To find out more about our authors and books visit www.bloomsbury.com. Here
you will find extracts, author interviews, details of forthcoming events and the
option to sign up for our newsletters.

Picture credits

Illustrations by Dave Saunders.
p11 © Crown Copyright 2015, adapted from image supplied by Met Office;
p37 (top) © Handout/Getty Images; p42 © DON EMMERT/AFP/Getty Images;
pp46–7 © NGA; p56, p59, pp91–9 © British Crown Copyright 2015, all rights
reserved; p120 © Will Imanse of Techs Mex Services in La Paz Mexico.
This product has been derived in part from material obtained from the UK
Hydrographic Office with the permission of the UK Hydrographic Office, Her
Majesty's Stationery Office. THIS PRODUCT IS NOT TO BE USED FOR NAVIGATION.
NOTE Every effort has been made to find the copyright holders of any
material used in this book that is not the author's own.

Introduction

- ◆ Navigation: the additional knowledge you need for long-distance navigation as opposed to coastal navigation
- ◆ Astro navigation: how to work out an astro sight, step-by-step, as a fall-back if GPS fails
- ◆ Yacht preparation: the important additions and modifications you may need to consider for your yacht before embarking on a long-distance voyage
- ◆ Heavy weather: practical advice on preparing for heavy weather on passage, and survival tactics
- ◆ Communication: the capabilities and limitations of radio and satellite communications technologies
- ◆ Passage making: planning and preparation for a long passage, and how to organise and manage the yacht and crew on passage
- ◆ Risks and emergencies: an overview of the risks and emergencies that you may need to deal with, and sensible precautions, including training and equipment

It is assumed that the reader is familiar with basic theory of navigation, weather etc up to Yachtmaster Offshore level, which may be found in the *Reeds Skipper's Handbook*.

Acknowledgements
My thanks to Ash Woods for his careful review of the manuscript, and to Lin Parker and Richard Andrew (Velvet Adventure Sailing) for their invaluable input – based on far greater experience than my own.

World temperature

The world is heated by the sun.

- In the tropics the direction of the sun is nearly perpendicular to the earth's surface so the heating effect is greatest here.
- Further towards the poles the surface is angled away from the direction of the sun; its energy is spread over a greater area so the heating effect is less.
- This pattern varies with the seasons, because the sun is overhead further to the north or south of the equator.

The effect of this is uneven, because:

- The surface of the land heats up and cools down more than the sea does.
- Warm or cold winds blow from one part of the world to another.
- Clouds shade the earth's surface from the sun.

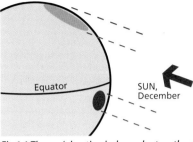

Fig 1.1 The sun's heating is dependent on the angle to the earth's surface.

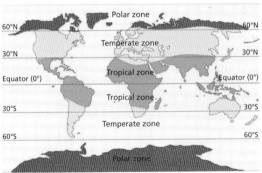

Fig 1.2 Climate zones.

Movement of air and Coriolis effect

The earth doesn't seem to us to be rotating, but it is – and that is what causes the Coriolis effect.

Imagine you are in London, and some 2,300NM north of you at the North Pole someone aims a missile towards you, travelling at 500 knots. If the earth wasn't rotating, it would come straight towards you, arriving 4 hours 36 minutes later. But as it is rotating:

◆ London would have moved 69° round to the east in that time. The missile would land in the middle of Quebec.
◆ If you were looking down from space you would see the missile travelling in a straight line, with the earth rotating beneath it.
◆ If you could watch it from London, you would see it curving off to the west instead of coming straight towards you.

The same is true of anything moving across a rotating earth – including the wind. Air moving in the northern hemisphere will experience a 'force' to the right of the direction of motion, due to the Coriolis effect. To get it to move in a constant direction (as seen on the rotating earth) you need a pressure gradient to counteract this 'force'.

Fig 1.3 shows what actually happens in the northern hemisphere.

The wind associated with straight isobars like this is called the geostrophic wind. The distance between isobars is an indication of the pressure gradient. Where the isobars are straight, you can use this distance to deduce the geostrophic wind speed. There is a scale printed on synoptic weather charts to enable you to do this.

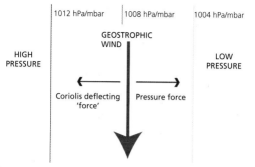

Fig 1.3 Geostrophic wind in the northern hemisphere.

In Fig 1.4, the geostrophic wind speed at the position shown (see the arrow on the left-hand side) is just under 25 knots. In practice, the wind at sea level is slightly slower than this, because of surface friction. Note that the scale – wind speed against pressure gradient –

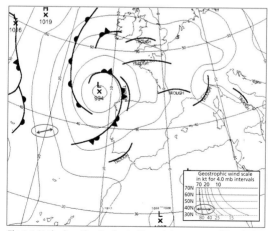

Fig 1.4 At the location indicated in red the geostrophic wind speed is just under 25 knots.

Movement of air and Coriolis effect

depends on latitude, because the Coriolis effect is greatest at the poles and zero at the equator.

Where is Coriolis strongest?

As you move further away from the pole, the earth's surface is not facing in the direction of the earth's rotational axis. It faces further and further 'outwards', until at the equator it is at 90° to the axis of rotation (see Fig 1.5).

So there is little or no Coriolis effect near the equator. Here, the surface of the earth is at right angles to the surface at the North Pole, and isn't rotating in the manner of a disc.

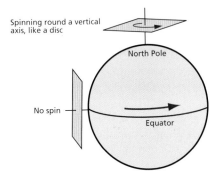

The Coriolis effect is strongest near the poles, reduces with latitude and is zero at the equator. It acts in the reverse direction in the southern hemisphere, because the spin direction is reversed.

Fig 1.5 The Coriolis effect.

Buys Ballot's Law

> In northern latitudes, face the wind and the barometer will be lowest to your right. In southern latitudes, face the wind and the barometer will be lowest to your left.

Buys Ballot's Law, above, conforms with Fig 1.3 showing geostrophic wind in the northern hemisphere.

Sailors in the North Atlantic and on European coasts will be well aware of the familiar example of a North Atlantic depression, shown in Fig 1.6. The circulation around it is anticlockwise; to the south of the low (where the warm and cold fronts generally are), winds are westerly.

Circulation around low pressure systems in the southern hemisphere is in the opposite direction: clockwise.

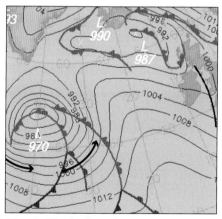

Fig 1.6 A typical North Atlantic depression, showing the wind direction.

World winds

World winds

The average wind direction in different parts of the world can be understood as an idealised pattern, which would exist on a 'perfect' world without land masses. This pattern is disrupted by the physical arrangement of oceans and landmasses, and by more random weather events.

Figure 1.7 shows the idealised pattern. It depicts the winds and atmospheric pressure at the earth's surface.

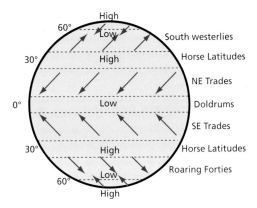

Fig 1.7 Idealised pattern of world winds and pressures.

In some cases the actual observed winds and surface pressures, in the open ocean, fit this pattern pretty well. During the year, the entire pattern moves north and south with the sun. There is a lot more land in the northern hemisphere than the southern, so in the south the observed fit with the idealised pattern is better.

Fig 1.8 shows how climatologists have modelled what is probably happening. The theory is based on

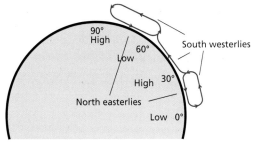

Fig 1.8 Vertical wind circulation (with the height above the earth exaggerated).

a vertical circulation pattern caused by heating and cooling at the earth's surface. The air flow is also influenced by the Coriolis effect; for example, south-moving air in the northern hemisphere turns to the west and becomes a north-easterly wind. Hence the north-east and south-east trades, the south-westerlies in northern temperate latitudes and the north-westerlies in the Roaring Forties.

All of this refers to average winds, which are overlaid by random small-scale events (ie weather). This weather overlay is more prevalent where frequent systems are generated by the meeting of different air masses, for example where the ocean and continents meet.

Important wind systems
Trade winds

These winds are good news for long-distance sailors and (as the name suggests) earlier commercial navigation by sail. In most areas of ocean, except where they are disrupted by other effects such as monsoons, the trade wind belt extends from about 30°N and 30°S latitudes towards the equator, until it meets the intertropical

Important wind systems

convergence zone. The area moves north and south slightly with the sun as the seasons change.

Wind blows predominantly from the north-east in the northern belt and south-east in the southern. Average wind speeds around the world are 13–18 knots. There are generally small, fluffy fair-weather cumulus clouds and blue sky.

> Actual wind direction varies between north and east (or south and east). Speed also varies as areas of high and low pressure interact with the general pattern. Winds can be quite fresh with speeds in the 20s, or can die away for a time to calm in thundery weather.

Doldrums: intertropical convergence zone (ITCZ)

It's a different story at the equator, where the northern and southern trade winds converge. Wind here is light and variable; you can expect calms, with thunderstorms and heavy tropical rain.

The ITCZ is an obstacle to sailing boats crossing between northern and southern hemispheres, so it is worth choosing a route where it is likely to be narrowest.

The ITCZ zone forms a slim roughly east–west belt near the equator, but its exact position is quite variable with the seasons, time and place. It is clearly defined in the Atlantic and Pacific, but in the Indian Ocean and China Seas it is disrupted in the summer by the monsoon.

In the western parts of the Atlantic and Pacific oceans the trade winds, north and south, tend to blow from a more easterly direction, and the ITCZ can be more innocuous as a result.

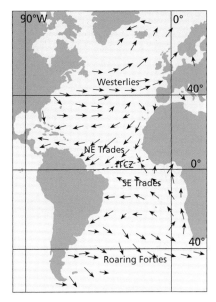

Fig 1.9 Average winds in the Atlantic in January.

Temperate zone: westerlies with mobile depressions

The idealised wind pattern (see Fig 1.7) gives south-westerly air flow between 35°N and 60°N, and north-westerly air flow between 35°S and 60°S in the 'Roaring Forties'. The average wind is indeed from these directions, but in both cases the actual wind is frequently disrupted by weather systems – mobile depressions and anticyclones – which tend to move from west to east. (Full descriptions of Atlantic depressions and associated fronts, and anticyclones, are covered in basic weather theory and are not repeated here – see *Reeds Skipper's Handbook* and *Reeds Weather Handbook*.)

Important wind systems

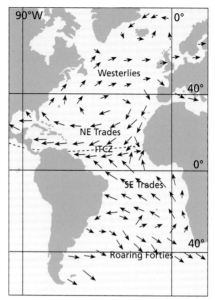

Fig 1.10 Average winds in the Atlantic in July.

In the northern hemisphere the zone is dominated by the presence of land, giving a local character to conditions in the Atlantic and Pacific oceans. In the southern hemisphere, however, this zone is more or less continuous around the world, and winds very often reach gale force, earning the region its name.

Subtropical high pressure belt

Between the trade wind belt and the temperate zone (about 30°N–35°N and 30°S–35°S) there is a predominantly high pressure area. Although occasionally disrupted by depressions, this area is characterised by light variable winds and fine weather. These are the

'Horse latitudes' – so called because in the light winds sailing ships on their way to America and the West Indies occasionally had to throw overboard their cargo of horses, owing to the shortage of water and fodder.

Monsoons

The biggest departure from the idealised wind pattern is caused by seasonal heating and cooling of large land masses – similar to daytime sea breezes on a hot day near the land, but on a far larger scale. Monsoons happen in the Indian Ocean, and are caused by the heating and cooling of the large Asian land mass.

In the summer, strong heating over Asia causes an extreme low pressure to develop there. This is caused by the ascent of air, heated at the surface, to the upper atmosphere. The resulting depression dominates the whole region and produces a south-west air flow from the equator up to the Indian and South-east Asian coast, and in the South and East China Seas (see Fig 1.11).

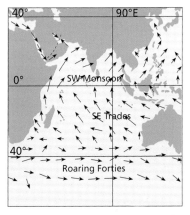

Fig 1.11 Average winds in the Indian Ocean in July.

Important wind systems

Winds in the Arabian Sea and Bay of Bengal are strong and stormy, and bring intense rainfall to coastal areas. These conditions persist from May to September.

In the winter, the opposite occurs. Intense cooling over Asia produces a huge area of high pressure as cold air subsides towards the surface. Clockwise circulation around this anticyclone produces a north-easterly air flow (see Fig 1.12). This is not as strong as the summer monsoon, and because the wind is blowing off the land, not as wet. Weather is generally fine and clear.

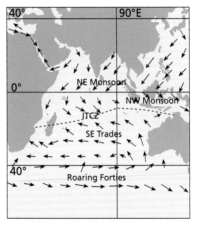

Fig 1.12 Average winds in the Indian Ocean in January.

As this air crosses the equator it changes direction, blowing towards the north coast of Australia as the north-west monsoon.

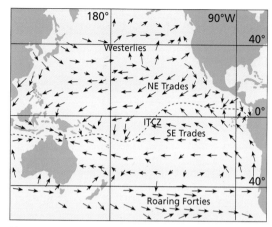

Fig 1.13 Average winds in the Pacific in January.

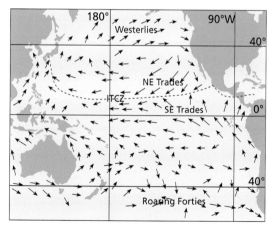

Fig 1.14 Average winds in the Pacific in July.

Local winds

When sailing near land, you can get locally generated winds, or a surprisingly sudden increase in the general gradient wind, caused by the flow of air past land features or strong heating/cooling of the land. These may be more pronounced than you are accustomed to in your home cruising ground, and it is worth being aware of their causes.

HEADLANDS AND ACCELERATION ZONES

Caused simply by the flow of the wind past land obstacles, you can get very local – and therefore very sudden – increase in wind speed, close to exposed headlands or downwind of mountainous areas. Where this effect is particularly pronounced it will normally be described in pilot books (see Fig 1.16).

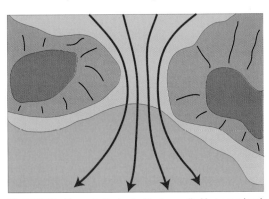

Fig 1.15 Wind funnel effect: wind is channelled between land features.

✷ Tip
When sailing along a coastline with an offshore breeze, keep a lookout ahead for white caps or other evidence of local strong wind – and shorten sail accordingly.

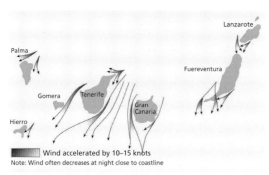

Wind accelerated by 10–15 knots
Note: Wind often decreases at night close to coastline

Fig 1.16 The Canary Islands acceleration zones.

SEA AND LAND BREEZES
These can occur anywhere in the world, particularly in hot climates where there is a greater diurnal variation of temperature.

KATABATIC WINDS
These winds occur near land, can be surprisingly strong, and are normally well-known locally.

When the earth cools by radiation, after sunset or at night, the air next to it cools and becomes denser.

Local winds

Where this occurs on sloping ground, gravity causes the heavier air to flow downhill and form a local wind, sometimes accelerated by a local funnel effect. If you read local pilot books, and listen to those with knowledge of the area, you will be forewarned; katabatic winds can be quite predictable, and generally die down after a few hours.

TORNADOS AND WATERSPOUTS

Tornados occasionally occur over the sea and form waterspouts. They are small areas of very strong wind circulation, with diameters from 1m to more than 100m.

Waterspouts are most likely to be found in tropical conditions, under heavy cumulonimbus cloud. A funnel-shaped cloud starts to extend downwards towards the sea, and at sea level the strong wind whips up a column of spray. Typically waterspouts last up to half an hour and travel quite slowly.

NAMED LOCAL WINDS

In certain localities there are weather conditions that give rise to a particular local (often strong) wind. Not unnaturally, the inhabitants have given these winds names, and it is useful for the long-distance sailor to be aware of what people, and local weather forecasts, may be warning you about.

In alphabetical order, here are brief descriptions of some well-known local winds that you may encounter. It's worth learning more about their characteristics, if you plan to visit these areas.

Bora: a cold, dry, katabatic, north to east wind, from the mountains of the north and east Adriatic. It is often sudden, with violent gusts.

Etesian: summer northerly wind of the Aegean Sea and eastern Mediterranean.

Gregale: a strong north-east wind found in the central and western Mediterranean, chiefly near Malta and Sicily. It occurs mainly in the winter, and is significant for harbours open to the north-east.

Harmattan: an easterly wind that blows from November to March off the west coast of Africa, between the Cape Verde islands and the Gulf of Guinea. It is a dry, relatively cool wind, with dust and sand from the Sahara.

Khamsin: a hot, dry, dusty and often strong southerly wind, in the Red Sea and Egypt. It occurs from February to June, most frequently in March and April.

✳ Tip
For practical advice on receiving local weather forecasts see page 140. Long distance sailing is as much about adapting to different localities, and being able to base decisions on local advice, as it is about crossing oceans.

Levanter: a damp easterly wind in the Strait of Gibraltar. It is usually only light or moderate, but when strong it can cause unpleasantly violent eddies in the lee of the Rock.

Mistral: a strong north or north-west wind which blows over the Gulf of Lion in the western Mediterranean. The wind is strengthened by the katabatic flow down the mountains, and by channelling down the Rhone valley;

Local winds

thus it frequently blows at gale force, and produces a rough sea. It is a cold, dry wind and the weather is usually sunny and clear.

Norther: a northerly winter gale in Chile, bringing rain. Also a strong, cool, dry north wind in the Gulf of Mexico and western Caribbean, also in the winter. It can come suddenly, and can reach gale force in the Gulf of Mexico.

Pampero: a weather event in the River Plate area. When a sharp cold front passes, with heavy rain and thunder, the wind backs suddenly from north to south or south-west and can become very severe during the first squall.

Sirocco: southerly wind in the Mediterranean. Hot and dry when it leaves the North African coast, damp and frequently foggy when it reaches the countries to the north.

Shamal: any north-west wind in the Persian Gulf and Gulf of Oman, varying to west along the coast. It brings dry air and a cloudless sky, but poor visibility because of sand and dust. In winter it can be gale force or more, and be accompanied by thundery rain squalls. In the summer it is less strong.

Southerly Buster: a violent squall behind a cold front in south-east Australia. The wind backs to south, and frequently reaches gale force.

Sumatra: squall from the south-west in the Malacca Straits and the west coast of Malaya. Sumatras are frequent between May and October, and often reach gale force, with thunder and torrential rain.

Ocean currents

In the oceans there is a pattern of currents – general movement of the water – which, on the surface, follow the main wind patterns in each ocean. However, the current circulation is quite complex, and can affect the water temperature, as cold water flows towards the tropics and vice versa. The flow is three-dimensional, but sailors are only affected by the surface current.

✳ Tip

When island-hopping in the Caribbean, don't get caught out by the strong west-going current that sets between the Windward Islands – or you may end up beating upwind to make it to your destination.

The term 'current' refers to this constant movement of water. This should not be confused with 'tidal stream', which is water movement caused by the tides. Tidal streams are of little consequence for ocean sailors because there is little or no tidal stream away from the land and even where they are experienced their effect cancels out over 12 hours. So when planning offshore passages of longer duration, they tend to be ignored (aside from departure and landfall).

Surface currents however are of interest, particularly on long passages. Where they are strong (eg the Gulf Stream, or the Aghulhas Current of south-east Africa), they can produce very rough conditions and steep waves in strong wind against the current. Where they are more benign, you can choose a route to take advantage of them. In all cases you need to be aware of the current for navigation – particularly with stronger currents, or if you are using estimated positions (EPs) with a long period between position fixes – using astro, for example.

Ocean currents

Detailed information on surface currents, based on observations, can be found on pilot charts.

Atlantic Ocean
NORTH ATLANTIC
The surface current pattern is dominated by a large clockwise circulation, similar to the prevailing winds.

A wide westerly flow below about 20°N (North Equatorial Current) is joined by a flow from the South Atlantic, and produces a strong westerly flow into the Caribbean Sea, and a strong concentrated flow (Gulf Stream) up the east coast of the United States. This turns into a north-easterly flow towards northern Europe (North Atlantic Current) and becomes less concentrated. The northern part of this flow continues past northern Scotland towards Scandinavia; while the southern part turns south, past the west coasts of Spain, Portugal and North Africa (Canary Current), to turn west again. In the centre of this circulation area, currents are weaker.

To the north of this main circulation, there is a smaller anticlockwise flow (Irminger Current) heading south-west past the south of Greenland and south down the west coast of Canada (Labrador Current). There is also an anticlockwise circulation between Scandinavia and Greenland.

SOUTH ATLANTIC
Here there is a large anticlockwise circulation. A wide westerly flow (South Equatorial Current) exists from just north of the equator to about 15°S. This splits when it reaches the coast of Brazil; the northern part turns north along the coast to join the North Atlantic circulation. The southern part becomes the Brazil Current, heading south-west along the coast.

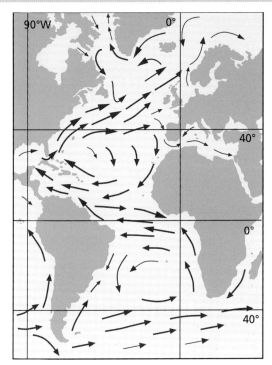

Fig 1.17 Atlantic Ocean currents.

At about the River Plate the Brazil Current meets the Falkland Current coming north-east, and turns south-east to join the broad Southern Ocean Current, heading eastwards, lying between about 40°S and 60°S. The northern part of the Southern Ocean Current turns north when it reaches the west coast of Africa (Benguela Current); the southern part continues past South Africa, into the southern Indian Ocean.

> Between North and South Atlantic main circulations there is the east-going Equatorial Counter Current, which becomes the Guinea Current flowing past Ivory Coast and Ghana, into the Gulf of Guinea.

Pacific Ocean

The Pacific is broadly similar to the Atlantic, with greater east–west extent. The differences seem to be attributable to the shape of the land round the edges.

In the North Pacific there is a large clockwise circulation, with weaker currents in its centre. The west-going North Equatorial Current lies between roughly 10°N and 20°N. Most of this flow turns north when it reaches the Philippines and flows north-east past Japan (Kuro Shio). It returns east (North Pacific Current and Aleutian Current) between latitudes 30°N and 50°N and south again (California Current) when it reaches North America. There is also an inshore current off California that flows in the opposite direction (north-west).

To the north of this large circulation there are two smaller anticlockwise ones: the Alaska Current in the Gulf of Alaska and in the Bering Sea, producing the south-west-flowing Kamchatka Current off the Kamchatka Peninsula.

In the South Pacific the west-going South Equatorial Current extends from just north of the equator to about 10°S. Most of this flow passes to the north of Australia, although some turns south as the East Australian Coast Current. The main Southern Ocean Current lies between 40°S and 55°S, and curves further south as it nears South America. It splits as it reaches the coast of Chile, and there is a strong north-going Peru Current from here, before it turns west again to join the South Equatorial Current.

Between the North and South Equatorial Currents, between about 5°N and 10°N, lies the east-going Equatorial Counter Current which recurves north-west when it reaches the coast of Central America.

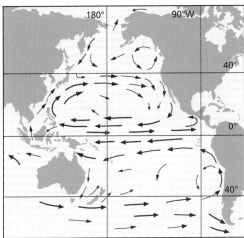

Fig 1.18 Pacific Ocean currents.

Indian Ocean

The Indian Ocean is slightly different. Currents in the northern part are seasonal, varying with north-east and south-west monsoon periods.

In the southern part of the ocean there is an anticlockwise circulation. A strong westerly flow exists between about 10°S and 20°S (South Equatorial Current); the southern half of this turns south when it reaches Madagascar and East Africa (Mozambique Current and Aghulhas Current), then joins the broad easterly flow of the Southern Ocean Current below 40°S.

Ocean currents

In the northern part, from the Seychelles Group north, the south-west monsoon in the northern summer produces a generally eastern flow. This sets all the way through the Arabian Sea and past Sri Lanka, but is less well defined in the north of the Bay of Bengal.

The north-east monsoon in the northern winter produces the opposite: a generally western flow north of the equator, and from the equator to about 10°S an east-going counter current.

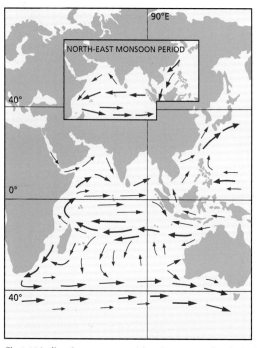

Fig 1.19 Indian Ocean currents (showing seasonal variation).

Tropical revolving storms

Tropical revolving storms, known as hurricanes in the Atlantic, cyclones in the Indian Ocean and South Pacific, or typhoons in the North Pacific, are the world's most violent weather system.

If you are planning to cross an ocean in a small boat, one of the most important considerations is to know when and where these are likely to occur, and so avoid being in the wrong area at the wrong time.

Fortunately their occurrence is seasonal and, up to a point, predictable. You might be unlucky with an early or late storm, but if you are reasonably conservative in your planning and steer clear of the known storm seasons, you can probably avoid them.

The storms themselves, once they occur, are less predictable in their behaviour.

✳ Tip
It's instructive to look at images and videos of tropical revolving storms on the internet. They will do nothing but increase your respect for (and desire to avoid) these incredible phenomena.

Formation
FORMATION CONDITIONS
◆ Storms are powered by warm ocean water; the sea temperature must be at least 26°C to a depth of 60m, and in practice nearer 28°C at the surface.
◆ Warm, moist air at sea level and cooler air at altitude, giving unstable, 'thunderstorm' conditions.
◆ To start the storm's rotation, there needs to be a Coriolis effect. This means that storms form at least 5° to 10° away from the equator.

31

Tropical revolving storms

◆ Formation is assisted by weak high-level winds, and by a weather disturbance (some form of tropical depression or wave).

FORMATION PROCESS

Heavy showers and thunderstorms are not uncommon in the tropics, and these (on a large scale) can sometimes initiate the formation of a TRS.

◆ The starting point is strong 'convection activity' (ie warm air rising). The air just above a very warm ocean is itself very warm and contains a lot of water vapour (water in its clear gaseous state) evaporated from the ocean, and this low density air rises.

◆ As the air rises, it expands in the lower pressure and cools itself. But in thunderstorm conditions, the upper air is cold, colder than the air rising up. This is known as an 'unstable' atmosphere, because instead of stopping, the warm air (with its water vapour) continues to rise.

◆ It also continues to cool, and eventually it cools to a point where the water vapour condenses into cloud and rain.

◆ To turn liquid water into gas, you have to heat it; conversely, when the gas turns back into liquid, you get the heat energy back (this is called latent heat). So the rising air suddenly starts to get more energy from the condensing water, which heats it up and makes it rise even more strongly in the surrounding colder air (see Fig 1.20).

◆ This process continues, with the latent heat of the condensing water powering ever stronger convection high into the atmosphere, and the condensed water falling as torrential rain.

1 Warm, moist air over the warm sea rises.

2 As it rises it cools – but it's still warmer than the surrounding air, so it goes on rising ('unstable' atmosphere).

3 Water vapour condenses into cloud and rain. This gives the air more heat energy (latent heat) and the air rises strongly.
  More warm moist air is drawn in from the surrounding ocean.

Fig 1.20 Convection, powered by latent heat.

If this happens over a wide area:

◆ Warm moist surface air from the surrounding ocean is drawn in to replace the rising air (see Fig 1.21).
◆ This air is also drawn upwards, joining the convection and bringing more latent heat energy with it.

So the whole thing becomes a sort of gigantic heat engine, with a limitless supply of 'fuel' in the form of warm, moisture-laden air from the surrounding ocean. (A storm moving over land decreases in strength, because it has lost this energy source.)

Tropical revolving storms

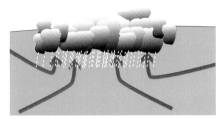

Fig 1.21 Warm, damp air is drawn in from a wide area of ocean.

◆ As air moves in from a wide area towards a small centre of strong convection and very low pressure, it starts to circulate because of the Coriolis effect (see Fig 1.22). In the northern hemisphere the wind blows to the right of the low pressure area, continually turning in towards it, to produce an anticlockwise circulation.

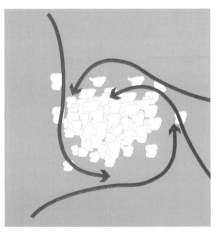

Fig 1.22 The Coriolis effect causes circulation to start (northern hemisphere shown here).

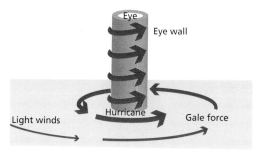

Fig 1.23 Winds intensify towards the eye.

♦ The circulating air is sucked towards the middle, and the whole system becomes a giant vortex. (Think of the vortex you get in still water when you take the bath plug out; now imagine the same thing, upside down, on a vast scale, with air being sucked high into the upper atmosphere.)

♦ As the air moves towards the centre of the vortex its circulation speeds up because of angular momentum (the way a spinning skater speeds up when she pulls her arms in).

♦ Wind speed increases towards the centre of the vortex, until you get to an inner circular 'wall' (see Fig 1.23). Here the wind speeds are highest, and the movement of air becomes more vertical. Inside the wall is the 'eye' of the storm, which has relatively light winds.

Structure of a developed storm

♦ Storms vary in size, but the storm shown in Fig 1.24 is reasonably typical.

♦ In the centre is the eye. This is a small area, 20–30NM wide, in which there are light winds and frequently clear sky. It's very distinctive in satellite pictures.

35

Tropical revolving storms

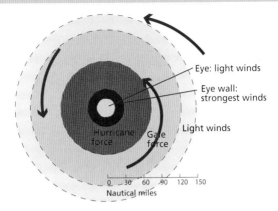

Fig 1.24 The structure of a mature storm. The arrows show wind direction (northern hemisphere), circulating and converging on the centre.

◆ Surrounding the eye is the 'eye wall', the area of strongest winds. Typically, winds of at least force 12 can extend to 75NM from the centre. Beyond that, winds of gale force typically extend for a further 40NM, beyond which lighter winds, force 6 say, are experienced.

◆ Bands of heavy cloud, convection activity and rain extend in spirals from the centre. The spirals of cloud can be seen in satellite photos.

Movement

Storms in both hemispheres tend to track initially to the west and away from the equator, averaging 8–10 knots. The typical paths of storms (based on actual observation) are shown on pilot charts.

At some stage they will start to recurve: north-west, north, north-east in the northern hemisphere, and the

Fig 1.25 Satellite image of typhoon.

mirror image in the south. At this stage they typically start to move faster, say 20–25 knots.

Unfortunately, it is difficult for forecasters to make reliable predictions of the movement and recurvature of these storms, and this makes them all the more dangerous.

Fig 1.26 2010 tropical storm tracks. Note the randomness of individual storm behaviour.

Tropical revolving storms

Avoidance and survival tactics

The primary tactic to avoid a TRS is not to be in the area of ocean at the time of year when they are liable to occur. (Most of us avoid them very successfully in this way.)

Commercial shipping does not have this luxury, so they have developed tactics to avoid/survive actual storms as best they can. These tactics are worth knowing about in case you ever get caught out in a small boat, but don't become complacent. These storms are extremely dangerous, even to large ships.

APPROACHING STORM

To receive warning of an approaching storm, and an indication of how it is likely to track, the obvious answer is, if possible, to access up-to-date accurate weather information, either from radio forecasts, weather fax, or satellite (see page 140). But there are other warning signs to look out for.

BAROMETRIC PRESSURE

In the tropics, there is a predictable 'diurnal' (daily) pattern of pressure variation of up to 1.5hPa/mbar above and below the mean pressure. Barometer readings need to be corrected to take account of this, if you wish to detect underlying – more worrying – trends. Correction tables, for each hour of local time, are published for this purpose.

◆ When the storm is 100–200NM away, there will be a slight drop in pressure which will only be detected by careful, systematic observation of the barometer reading.

◆ When the storm is closer, the fall in barometric pressure is more marked and will be discernable without taking the diurnal variation into account. But by this time the centre of the storm may only be 60–120NM away.

WEATHER AND CLOUD
◆ Initially, extensive cirrus cloud, often in convergent bands towards the storm's centre, strongly coloured at sunset and sunrise
◆ Later, a thick layer of altostratus (high solid grey cloud)
◆ Eventually, lower cloud, accompanied by heavy rain squalls

Initially rain is intermittent and showery. As the centre of the storm approaches, the rain becomes torrential.

DANGEROUS AND 'NAVIGABLE' SEMICIRCLES
If a storm is coming towards you, the winds in front of it are blowing across the storm's path; on one side, the wind is blowing towards the track and, on the other side, away from it. The side where winds are blowing you towards the likely path of the centre of the storm is also the side where the storm may turn towards you if it recurves (see Fig 1.27).

Because of this, one half of the storm is termed the 'dangerous semicircle', and the other side 'navigable', although one should take the latter term with a pinch

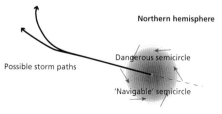

Fig 1.27 Dangerous and 'navigable' semicircles.

Tropical revolving storms

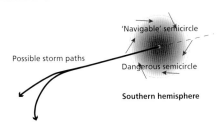

Fig 1.28 Dangerous and 'navigable' semicircles.

of salt. The winds are just as strong, it's just that it may be slightly easier to use them to get away from the path of the storm and avoid the worst of it.

WIND DIRECTION AND STORM PATH

If a storm is approaching and you are close enough to be affected by the circulating winds, you need to observe the change in wind direction to work out which side of its track you are on.

In the northern hemisphere, if you are on the 'dangerous' side of the track the wind will veer (change direction clockwise) as the storm approaches, and on the 'navigable' (ie marginally less dangerous) side, winds will back.

In the southern hemisphere, it's the other way round. A backing wind means you're on the 'dangerous' side and a veering wind means you're on the 'navigable' side.

SAILING TACTICS

The idea is to avoid the centre of the storm at all costs as it proceeds along its track.

In the northern hemisphere
- If the wind veers, you are on the dangerous side of the approaching storm. Try to avoid being blown towards the track of the storm centre, eg by heaving to, or sailing close-hauled on the starboard tack away from the storm centre, following the wind round as it veers.
- If the wind direction is steady (you are in the path of the storm) or backing (you are on the 'navigable' side), put the wind on the starboard quarter and reach/run out of the way of the storm, altering course to port as the wind backs.

In the southern hemisphere
The same logic applies:
- Backing wind: dangerous side, so heave to or climb upwind on port
- Steady or veering wind: reach or run with the wind on the port quarter

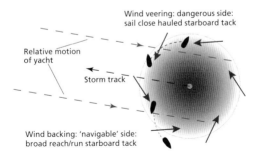

Wind veering: dangerous side:
sail close hauled starboard tack

Relative motion of yacht

Storm track

Wind backing: 'navigable' side:
broad reach/run starboard tack

Fig 1.29 Storm tactics (northern hemisphere).

Tropical revolving storms

LAND-BASED TACTICS

Long-distance sailors often spend the hurricane season with their yachts laid up ashore, or in safe 'hurricane hole' anchorages, in parts of the world that may be affected by storms. If you plan to do this, try to find:

◆ Locations that are less likely to be affected by storms (usually between 5°N and 5°S).
◆ Boatyards that have a proven capability of looking after yachts ashore (one method is to dig a trench for the keel so that the hull rests on solid ground).

However 'sheltered', anchorages are unlikely to be comfortable places in a storm. The advice is:

◆ Find a very sheltered anchorage with minimal fetch for waves to build up.
◆ Lie well away from other boats, or potential wind-borne debris.
◆ Attach the boat to shore with several lines to trees, mangroves etc.

Fig 1.30 If you face any chance of encountering a storm, do seek more detailed advice and local knowledge.

Route planning

Long-distance sailing trips start off as ideas or dreams. Perhaps you own a yacht, and long to sail it further than you are able to on summer holidays; perhaps you have an ambition to sail across a particular ocean, or visit a particular part of the world.

If you want to turn this into reality, you need to start by considering the following:

◆ Where do you want to go?
◆ How much time have you got?
◆ How quickly do you want to travel?
◆ How much time do you want to spend in each area?

This develops into a route plan, which includes:

◆ Consideration of when (season) you want to be where (sea/cruising area)
◆ Conditions expected for the longer passages, and any seasonal constraints (eg avoiding tropical storm seasons)
◆ Likely duration of the longer passages

The key to a successful route is to be in the right place at the right time, and in particular to make the longer passages at a suitable time of year. It's helpful to look at successful routes that other sailors have followed, for example:

◆ Typical world circumnavigations, planned over two or three years
◆ A one-year circuit around the North Atlantic

Your own route can borrow ideas from these and use parts of them. It's up to you to decide where you want to go and how hard you want to sail. Once you have chosen your route, you can start the planning and preparation for its specific challenges, and the more thoroughly you do this the more successful it is likely to be.

Route planning checklist

◆ Where do I want to go to?

◆ How far is it?

◆ How long will it take, allowing time for slow progress and bad weather?

◆ Can I do it in the time I have available/allocated?

◆ What will weather be like? Is there a time not to go?

◆ What kind of clothing and protection will I need for myself and my crew?

◆ What will wave height be like? How comfortable a passage will that make it?

◆ How many crew will I take?

◆ How much water will we need?

◆ Can we store enough food?

◆ Do we need extra electricity-generating equipment?

◆ How much diesel will we need?

◆ How much gas will we need?

◆ What will we do in very light airs?

◆ Are we allowed to go where we want to go?

◆ Do we need visas?

◆ Does the boat need special boat papers/documentation and where can we get these?

◆ Are there any local regulations/stipulations?

◆ Are there any high-risk areas that ought to be avoided, because of military conflict, political instability, the threat to personal safety/health, or piracy?

These questions will guide your decisions for equipping and preparing your yacht.

Information sources
Pilot charts

Pilot charts are an indispensable source of the type of information you need for route and passage planning.

They are not hugely expensive, and they don't go out of date. A good chart agent should stock them, and these days you can also download them free from the internet in PDF format.

These charts are published for each ocean (North and South Atlantic, North and South Pacific, Indian), with other areas of interest (Mediterranean, Caribbean) put in as additional sections or inserts. There is a chart for each month of the year, with the following information, mostly gathered as actual observations over many years:

Magnetic variation: lines of equal magnetic variation, sometimes including annual rate of change.

Great circle routes: shortest distance routes, avoiding any seriously adverse conditions for the month.

Wave heights: lines of equal percentage frequency of large waves (sea and swell), and notes on monthly trend.

Wind roses: for each 5° lat/long square, there is a wind 'rose' that indicates the percentage recorded occurrence of winds from different directions, together with their average strengths. There is also a figure for percentage of calms.

Gales: for each 5° square, the percentage of ships' reports of gale force winds or higher, plus accompanying notes about areas subject to gales for the month.

Extratropical cyclones (such as Atlantic lows): notes about the areas where they are generated and likely paths for the month.

Information sources

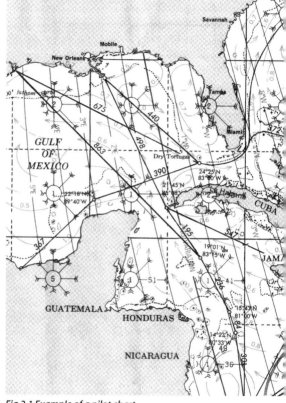

Fig 2.1 Example of a pilot chart.

Tropical cyclones: indication of average tracks of tropical revolving storms in each month, and notes on the storm season and frequency of storms for the month shown.

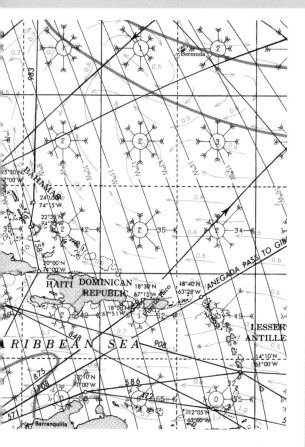

Air temperature: lines of equal mean air temperature and accompanying notes.

Sea surface temperature: lines of equal sea surface temperature.

Information sources

Atmospheric pressure: notes about main pressure features (eg Azores High) for the month, plus lines of equal average pressure.

Visibility: lines indicating the percentage frequency of poor visibility, and notes on problem areas for the month.

Ocean currents: comprehensive information on the prevailing direction and speed of surface currents.

Ice: ice limits (mean, maximum, minimum) and mean maximum iceberg limit for the month.

What you need
All this information is useful, but for initial planning of a relatively benign cruising route you will be mainly concerned with:

◆ **Tropical cyclones**: avoid the season, and if you can't, avoid the area where they may form and track.
◆ **Wave heights**: these charts give a very quick appreciation of the likely occurrence of rough weather, so you can quickly see the calmer months for a particular passage.
◆ **Wind direction**: this is a key factor for sailing. The charts will quickly show you the trade winds, for example.

Route planning books
Pilot charts may be regarded as 'raw information', which is tailored for the most part to the needs of commercial shipping. Other publications are aimed specifically at cruising sailors.

Essentially these are based on actual experiences of people who have done it before, on similarly sized boats, so it is sensible (and somewhat reassuring) to use this information to sail similar routes, at similar times of the year, to what has worked successfully in the past.

As well as getting good advice on the climate and conditions, when to go and not to go, you get ideas and advice on how to structure desirable world cruising routes to fit in with the seasons.

One such publication is *World Cruising Routes*, by Jimmy Cornell; another, specifically for the Atlantic, is *The Atlantic Crossing Guide*, by Jane Russell. *World Cruising Routes* covers all the oceans, includes hundreds of routes, and for each, advises waypoints and distances, conditions to expect, best times to make the passages, etc.

There are other similar publications, and many accounts by long-distance sailors, and it is well worth tapping into their experience.

✳ Tip
You tend to build on your knowledge of routes, passages and experiences in conversation with other sailors you meet along the way.

Organised rallies
An alternative that many long-distance sailors prefer is to join an organised rally. There are many rallies available, round-the-world or across a single ocean. They vary in their aims and style; some are simply cruising rallies whose primary purpose is to give help and encouragement to less experienced ocean skippers and crews. Others have developed into racing events. In general, they may feature:

◆   Practical advice on safety and passage planning
◆   Individual yacht inspections prior to the event

Information sources

- ◆ Social gatherings before and after a passage
- ◆ Satellite tracking of yachts
- ◆ On-passage weather advice
- ◆ Radio nets

Costs vary, and may well include access to negotiated group rates at starting and finishing marinas.

Rallies can be an excellent stepping stone for ordinary yachtsmen, to enable them do something extraordinary: cross an ocean. At the same time you should remember that with ocean sailing there is no such thing as 'safety in numbers'. At sea you are on your own, and you need to take responsibility for this. You shouldn't see the rally as an excuse. A good skipper should be well-informed and self-sufficient.

It's attractive to embark on your route with a group of people you will get to know. This can be particularly valuable for children. Having said that, it's pretty easy to make friends and form informal 'cruising groups' if you travel independently of a rally (particularly if you have an SSB radio), and this way you retain the flexibility of going where you want, when you want.

Charts and pilot books

Once you have planned your route, it's time to give some thought to the detailed navigation information you are going to need along the way.

CHARTS

Charts are produced in a variety of formats and styles, by different agencies all over the world. You also have a choice between electronic and paper. It's probably easier to source the charts you need at home, before you go.

If you rely on electronic charts, you are dependent on a reliable chart plotter (or other display device) and electric power. For longer passages, in particular, it is wise to carry a paper chart as a back-up, in case your navigation system or electric power fails.

Because of the expense of charts, and the duration of their voyages, long-distance sailors tend to be fairly pragmatic about the charts they use. With experience you learn to get by with charts that are perhaps a smaller scale than you would ideally prefer, and that may not be fully up-to-date.

✳ Tip

If you are using a chart that hasn't been updated with the latest corrections, be aware of what might have changed (light characteristics, navigation marks, 'human' features) and what almost certainly hasn't (coastlines, rocks). You may have been taught always to use fully up-to-date charts, but for hundreds of years navigators didn't have that luxury, and had to sound their way cautiously into unknown waters. It's not a bad thing to rediscover those skills rather than place too much reliance and confidence in a chart that may be in error.

PILOT BOOKS/CRUISING GUIDES

Pilot books are an invaluable source of cruising information, and the detailed large-scale plans of harbour approaches and anchorages can compensate for the rather small-scale chart you used to get there. Like charts, they are not cheap, and it's worth getting the most up-to-date information you can – ports and facilities can change quite quickly in popular areas.

Ocean navigation

Ocean navigation

The navigation theory for coastal and offshore sailing still applies to ocean sailing, but there are other factors to be aware of when sailing longer passages, or sailing further from familiar home waters.

◆ The **shortest distance to your destination** is not necessarily a straight line on the chart. You need to understand why, when it is significant, and about different chart projections.

◆ **Magnetic compass**. Variation (the difference between true north and magnetic north) can be quite a bit larger than in European waters, and will frequently change during an ocean passage. You need to know how variation is presented on ocean charts. Additionally deviation (inaccuracy of the ship's compass) is more important on longer passages.

◆ **World standard times** and **time zones** are explained here, as longer passages frequently extend across time zone boundaries.

◆ **Satellite navigation systems** (such as GPS), now the primary means of navigation for ocean sailors, have done more than anything else to open up long-distance sailing to the average amateur sailor. Ocean sailors place considerable reliance on GPS, so it's a good idea to understand the factors that affect its accuracy and reliability.

Great circles

A great circle is the biggest circle you can draw on the surface of a sphere – the centre of the circle is at the centre of the sphere. The path along a great circle is the shortest distance between two points on the surface of the sphere, which is why it's important for navigation.

Examples of great circles on the earth are:

◆ All north–south meridian lines (lines of equal longitude, that run through both poles)
◆ The equator

Apart from the equator, lines of equal latitude are not great circles.

If you take a globe, you can stretch a piece of string or rubber band across it between two points, and that will show you the great circle route (see Fig 3.1). The taut string, showing the shortest distance, does not follow the east–west line; it curves to the north of it.

In practice, planned sailing routes are very much influenced by the expected conditions and prevailing winds; and actual routes are often dictated by the weather on passage. But you should be aware of the shortest distance route.

Fig 3.1 Great circle between Lisbon and Washington DC, which are both close to latitude 39°N.

Chart projections

Chart projections

The problem with charts is that they are printed on flat sheets of paper (or displayed on flat chart plotter screens), but the world is not flat: it's spherical. So although small areas of the earth's surface are nearly flat, once you try to map larger areas you start to run into difficulties. You have to 'distort reality' in order to represent a three-dimensionally curved surface on a flat piece of paper.

There are many different methods for doing this, and they are called map (or chart) projections. Each projection produces maps and charts that are distorted in one way, in order to be accurate (or useful) in another. So different projections suit different purposes.

Mercator projection

The projections mostly used for navigational charts are Mercator or transverse Mercator. These charts have the following properties:

a) Latitude and longitude (meridian) lines are straight, and (with very few exceptions) are printed parallel to the edges of the chart.

b) A straight line drawn on the chart is a line of constant direction (bearing from true north); the line crosses all the meridian lines at the same angle.

c) To achieve a) and b), the chart scale increases with latitude. The meridian lines, which in reality converge in higher latitudes, are drawn parallel on the chart, and the scale (in both directions) is adjusted to allow this to happen. (As a result, northern lands such as Greenland are shown disproportionately large on Mercator projection maps and charts.)

d) The shortest distance between two points (the great circle line) is not generally a straight line on the chart. The only exceptions are north–south meridian lines and the equator, which are great circles.

Chart projections

For the mariner, a) is useful because it facilitates plotting and reading off positions in latitude and longitude; and b) is useful because a course of constant compass heading can be plotted, or bearing line drawn, as a straight line on the chart. This is called a rhumb line.

The change of scale, c), is a minor inconvenience. On large-scale (small-area) charts it is barely noticeable, but on small-scale charts (eg extending 60NM or more) you need to be careful. When you measure off a distance on the chart, use the latitude scale, on the sides of the chart, close to the latitude of the distance you are measuring. The scale will be correct there, but not quite correct further north or further south on the chart.

The final point, d), is not significant for short passages; usually it is convenient, and perfectly good practice, to plot a course of constant direction relative to true north, ie a straight line on the chart. It is only for much longer distances that the great circle route becomes relevant: for this kind of planning we need a different chart projection.

Gnomonic projection

The other projection used by mariners is the gnomonic. The shape of the land and oceans is recognisable and undistorted near the central point, but this projection does not have the advantages of Mercator. It's harder to read off latitude and longitude or distance, for example. The chart becomes more distorted at the edges.

The sole advantage to the mariner is that a straight line on this chart is a great circle. So a straight line between A and B, on the gnomonic chart, is the shortest distance.

Chart projections

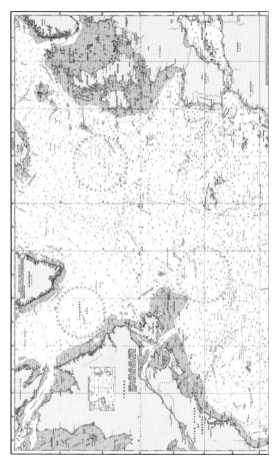

Fig 3.2 The North Atlantic, Mercator projection (British Crown Copyright 2015, all rights reserved).

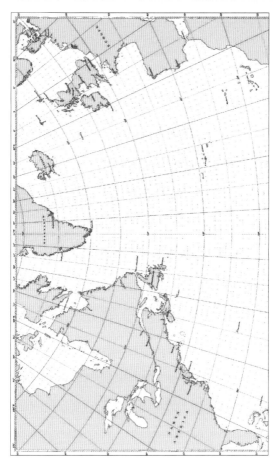

Fig 3.3 The North Atlantic, Gnomonic projection.

Chart projections

How important are great circles?

It's a good idea in planning a passage route to be aware of the path of least distance – or to put it another way, not to be misled by the straight rhumb line that you can draw to your destination on a Mercator chart.

In some circumstances rhumb lines are pretty close to great circles:

◆ If your passage is close to the equator
◆ If your passage has a significant north–south component

The great circle route is significant for passage planning when the passage is:

◆ Long
◆ Largely east–west
◆ At middle or high latitudes

✳ Tip

For many passages, the great circle is pretty irrelevant. The classic route from Europe to the Caribbean, for example, is head south until you reach the trade winds, then turn west to your destination. The GPS will give you the westerly great circle route, which in any case is close to the rhumb line at this latitude. You hardly need a gnomonic chart for this.

Navigation computers

Most navigation computers (eg on your GPS) will give you the great circle route from one waypoint to another. You can check this by entering two waypoints at, say, A at 50°N 0°W and B at 50°N 90°W. The course from A to B should not be 270°T – it should be 307°T. This represents the initial course to set off on, and it will change as you

Magnetic variation and deviation

proceed along the route. So even without a gnomonic chart you can easily obtain the great circle course when you need it.

Magnetic variation and deviation

Another feature of long-distance sailing is that:

◆ You may encounter larger magnetic variations than you are used to, eg several tens of degrees.
◆ The variation will change as you move across an ocean.

For this second reason, small-scale ocean charts do not have the compass roses you see on larger-scale charts, with the magnetic inner scale. Instead, they have lines showing 'contours' of equal magnetic variation, at 1° or 2° intervals (see Fig 3.4). The annual change is also shown, in brackets. Apart from this, you treat variation in exactly the same way for coastal sailing.

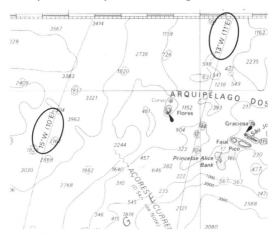

Fig 3.4 Magnetic variation shown on a small scale chart: magenta contours with annotations, as indicated.

Time

Deviation of the steering compass is frequently ignored for short passages, because the errors it causes aren't significant on a relatively short passage with a number of course changes. However, on a passage of 2,000NM on broadly the same heading, it could be significant. It is good practice to calibrate the compass for deviation before a long trip. Additionally, it can be checked on passage with astro navigation techniques (see page 106).

Time

Measurement of time, and time zones, can cause some confusion when sailing to different parts of the world. Time is also fundamental to navigation, particularly to the determination of longitude.

Measurement

Since pre-history, time has been measured by the passage of the sun. If you have a sundial, you can determine where you are in the 24-hour day; with the sun telling you when it is noon, or mid-day (sun at its highest), and the dial calibrated in hours before and after noon.

But then someone invented the clock, and it started to get more complicated:

◆ It was discovered that the sun isn't as good at keeping time as an accurate clock is.
◆ As travel and communication got faster, it became necessary to establish an agreed standard time with people to the east or west of you.

So clocks are set according to the average (mean) time at which the sun crosses the Greenwich Meridian. This Greenwich Mean Time (GMT) has been adopted as the basis for the world's standard reference time, known as Universal Time (UT).

Time

The sun actually crosses the Greenwich Meridian at anything between 11.44 GMT and 12.14 GMT, depending on the time of year. The difference between GMT and the sun's meridian passage at Greenwich is called the equation of time, and is tabulated for each day of the year in *The Nautical Almanac*. The equation of time is the same at all other meridians as it is at Greenwich.

If you need to work out the time of the sun's meridian passage time at your particular longitude (eg for a noon sight of the sun to determine latitude) you include the equation of time in your calculation (see page 73).

✳ **Tip**
A lot of publications (eg almanacs, *Admiralty List of Radio Signals*) and international radio services are based on UT. So it's useful to keep one clock on board set permanently to UT – it eliminates any confusion as you travel to different time zones.

Time zones and standard times

Everyone around the world wants to use a time that roughly agrees with their own local 'sun' time, but we also want to convert easily to UT and other people's time. For this reason the world has been divided into 24 time zones, each with its own standard time one hour different between adjacent zones.

Dividing 360° by 24, you get 15° of latitude per zone. Thus each zone is roughly centred on the 15°, 30°, 45°, 60°… meridians, east and west of Greenwich, although there are local variations to suit local geography and political considerations. The standard times in these zones are 1–11 hours before or after UT.

Time

There is a convention for naming time zones:

◆ Going to the east of Greenwich, with standard times ahead of UT, the zones are –1, –2 etc.
◆ In the westerly direction the zones are named +1, +2 etc.

✳ Tip
To take an example, in zone –2, you subtract two hours from the standard time to get UT.
Remember:

◆ The sun rises in the east, so the day starts earlier to the east.
◆ 'Plus is west' on this time zone naming convention.

The International Date Line is centred on the 180° meridian, with a number of kinks to suit the territories close to the meridian. The time zone is +12/–12:

◆ On the east (American) side of the line the standard time is 12 hours behind UT.
◆ On the west (Siberian, New Zealand) side it is 12 hours ahead of UT, on the subsequent day.

The Nautical Almanac contains a useful list of places and their standard times, before or after UT.

'Daylight savings' or 'summer' time is implemented in a number of countries round the world. The custom in these countries is to advance their standard time by one hour during the summer months.

Thus in the Greenwich time zone, in the UK, 12.00 UT becomes 13.00 BST from about the beginning of April until the end of October. Australian daylight savings time is typically in operation from early October to early April. An incidental result of this arrangement is that the London–Sydney time difference is nine hours in London summer and eleven hours in Sydney summer. It is very rarely the time zone difference of ten hours.

Time and longitude

If you are trying to work out where you are by looking at the celestial bodies, the task is complicated by the fact that the world is spinning very fast on its axis. Suppose you are out on the ocean taking sights on the sun to fix your position. You take some sights; and two minutes later another boat, 30 minutes of longitude due west of you, could be taking exactly the same sights. This means that, if you want to know how far east or west you are (your longitude) you need to know the time pretty accurately. Four seconds of time can make one nautical mile of difference to your calculated position.

This notorious problem for mariners was solved first by John Harrison's invention of the first serviceable chronometer, and ultimately overcome by radio, by which accurate time signals could be received at sea. Nowadays an ordinary electronic watch can be used to maintain accurate time on board, and can be checked regularly against the GPS or radio time signals. You can note how fast or slow it is in the log.

GPS is also reliant on accurate time. To calculate its position, the receiver has to know exactly where the fast-moving satellites are in relation to the earth (see page 64). The GPS system maintains and broadcasts very accurate (around 40ns) time information, and this can be displayed by the receiver.

Satellite navigation systems

Satellite navigation systems

The proper term for these systems is Global Navigation Satellite Systems (GNSS). There are currently two systems in service (the USA's GPS and the Russian GLONASS), with a third – Europe's Galileo system – due to become fully operational fairly soon. Some receivers are compatible with more than one system.

The most widely used and best known is the American Global Positioning System – GPS. This has been used by sailors since the early 1990s, and is now used by just about everyone with a clever mobile phone or in-car navigation system.

How GPS works

The Global Positioning System consists of 24 satellites orbiting the earth at a height of about 26,000km. The orbits are arranged so that there are at least four satellites visible at all times, at any point on the earth.

Each satellite broadcasts information that allows a receiver to calculate the satellite's position, to within 20m. It also transmits a signal at very precise, pre-determined times. With its internal clock, the receiver can work out how long the signal took to reach it, and therefore work out the distance to the satellite:

distance = (flight time) x (speed of light).

Knowing the distance to just three satellites will allow the receiver to work out its three-dimensional position (latitude, longitude, height). However, the principal inaccuracy is the receiver's own clock. If the receiver can acquire four or more satellites, it can improve the accuracy of the position significantly, by using the redundancy of information (rather like taking more compass bearings to improve the accuracy of your fix). If operating with fewer than the ideal number of satellites, the receiver can work out a two-dimensional fix, to limited accuracy, by assuming you are at sea level.

Satellite navigation systems

Accuracy and limitations
With enough satellites acquired, the accuracy of position by GPS is about 10m.

MILITARY SYSTEM
GPS is a military system that permits civil use. In its early days, the US military deliberately downgraded the accuracy available to civil (or foreign military) users, to 100m or so. This was known as 'selective availability', but it was withdrawn in 2000, allowing the current increased level of accuracy.

From time to time military forces conduct exercises that involve jamming the GPS in a particular area. In the UK, you can request prior notification of these exercises. In areas and times of serious military operations, it's anybody's guess what would happen.

ERRORS
The system is relatively free of errors, although as ever with navigation, you should make it a habit to check different sources of information against each other.

There is one distinct source of error: if your receiver picks up a satellite signal that has bounced off something, it will calculate the satellite range incorrectly. This can happen if you are close to a steep cliff, and perhaps if the direct path to the satellite is obstructed – in a fjord, for example.

Beyond this the most likely sources of error lie with the user.

CHART ACCURACY
In many areas – particularly those not frequented by international commercial shipping, where there is little demand for up-to-date surveys – the latitude and longitude scale on charts can be highly inaccurate. This is because the original survey did not have the benefit of

Satellite navigation systems

GNSS; it was most likely based on sextant observations. Your GPS position is considerably more accurate than the chart.

The moral is not to place too much trust in the latitude and longitude on the chart, particularly those based on 19th-century surveys. Use conventional pilotage techniques, and keep a good lookout for coral reefs – they may have grown a few metres in a couple of hundred years.

WHAT GPS DOES, AND DOESN'T DO

There is a fundamental limitation of GPS that is not immediately obvious if you are used to the extensive navigation functionality built into a GPS receiver and/or chart plotter. A single GPS receiver senses position only. It cannot detect direction or speed; these are calculated from previous positions that the navigation computer has 'remembered'.

If you use functions that show the speed and/or direction of the boat, unless your system incorporates an electronic compass, the 'direction' will be worked out from the last few positions of the GPS receiver. It will be usable provided the boat's motion is relatively steady, and will indicate track direction rather than heading.

Some vessels are equipped with a device called a GPS compass or satellite compass. This does sense direction: it has two or more GPS receivers, mounted some distance apart within the device, and calculates the true direction between their respective GPS positions.

USING GPS

GPS is incredibly easy to use – you can simply read off the latitude and longitude from the display and plot it on the chart (or get the chart plotter to do that automatically).

Points to note

◆ GPS receivers have a selection of chart datums that you can choose in the navigation setup menu. It is important to use the same datum that the chart uses, although this is only significant with relatively large-scale charts, close to land. Crossing an ocean you would not notice the error.

◆ It is easy enough to make a mistake taking numbers off a GPS display, or entering waypoint positions, so:

● Get into the habit of writing the position in the log before plotting it. This creates a proper record of the position fix (with time and log reading) and makes it easier to track down an error.

● When you are plotting the position, cross-check it against the logged distance and heading from the previous fix.

● When you enter a waypoint by keying in its latitude/longitude position, make sure that it 'makes sense'. Have a quick look at its range and bearing from your present position, or from another waypoint, to spot any gross error.

RECEIVER FAULTS

GPS receivers are made by independent manufacturers that use published GPS specifications to design their kit. How well the receivers work depends on how they are

Satellite navigation systems

designed, developed, tested and manufactured. Given the degree of reliance that can be placed on these devices, it is worth knowing that they can have software 'bugs' and design faults.

WEEK NUMBER ROLL-OVER
When the time is coded into messages from a GPS satellite, the system uses its own time scale, consisting of weeks and seconds from a particular start point. The week number goes from 0 to 1023, and then 'rolls over' to 0 again (because there are ten bits in the time code for the week number). When this last happened in August 1999, quite a few receivers failed to cope with it.

Some GPS receivers can be 'reset' by following a certain procedure, similar to re-booting a computer. This may solve the problem if the receiver software fails during roll-over, so it is worth knowing how to do it.

✳ Tip
The morning after GPS week number roll-over in August 1999, I heard a yacht calling to Brixham Coastguard for assistance in fixing their position. They were carrying two GPS receivers on board, one of which had been bought a week earlier because of this problem, and both had failed. The next week number roll-over event is on **6 April 2019**.

Before GPS became generally available in the early 1990s, astro navigation was the only method of position fixing available to yachtsmen on ocean passages. It was therefore a crucially important skill. Today satellite navigation is the primary means of position fixing for the vast majority of long-distance sailors. However, GPS is dependent on:

◆ Electric power
◆ Sensitive and complex electronic equipment, which cannot be repaired at sea

If your GPS fails when you are out of sight of land for whatever reason (eg water damage), astro navigation can still provide a position fix, and is the only method of doing so that requires no electronics.

✳ Tip
The VHF radio can sometimes be helpful if you are uncertain of your position:

◆ If you see another vessel, you can ask them to give you a position.
◆ If you are close enough to contact the coast-guard, they can measure the approximate bearing of your signal from one or more shore-based antennae.

The aim here is to give you enough information to:

◆ use a sextant to take a sight
◆ perform a sight reduction

It is assumed here that you require astro navigation purely as a fall-back and it will not be your primary method of navigation.

What you need

What you need
◆ A sextant
◆ An accurate watch
◆ *The Nautical Almanac* for the current year

The position fix can be plotted straight on to a small-scale ocean chart.

✳ Tip
Sextants needn't be expensive. Plastic ones are available, and there is a useful second-hand trade in those, and in high-quality metal ones. You need one that is accurate and in good repair as it's necessary to measure to the nearest minute of arc.

✳ Tip
Modern electric watches, or good-quality clockwork ones, are easily accurate enough to give you the time to the nearest second, provided you keep a note of how fast/slow they are, and how many seconds they gain/lose in a day.

Sight reduction methods
In order to obtain a position line from an astro sight, you need to perform a fairly complex calculation of the sun's (or other body's) altitude (angle above the horizon) and azimuth (bearing from true north). This can be done with a calculator, which is probably the quickest and easiest method. However, if your GPS has run out of power or is under a foot of water, it's just possible that your calculator or laptop might have suffered

the same fate. The alternative is to use tables, which require no electrics, but a little extra work with pencil and paper.

The method described below uses the concise sight reduction table. I've chosen this because:

◆ A pencil and paper method, using no electronics, is the surest 'fall-back' method in case of GPS failure.
◆ Speed is not really an issue, because this is not your normal or primary method of position fixing.
◆ *The Nautical Almanac* contains a copy of this table. Although alternatives exist, this is the most convenient option because you need a copy of *The Nautical Almanac* in any case.

How astro sights work

✳ Tip
You have to be able to see the horizon when using a normal sextant, ie it needs to be daylight, dusk or very bright moonlight. Also, do not try to measure a body that is almost overhead; it is too difficult to get an accurate result.

◆ With the sextant, you measure the vertical angle (altitude) from the horizon to the celestial body you choose: sun, moon, planets or star (see Fig 4.1).
◆ You note as accurately as possible the time when that measurement is made.

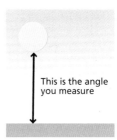

This is the angle you measure

Fig 4.1

How astro sights work

◆ You make some small corrections to the measured angle (using tables).
◆ For a position close to where you are (called the assumed position), you then calculate:
   ● The body's predicted altitude at the time of the sight
   ● Its azimuth (bearing) from the assumed position
   (This is the complicated bit, requiring quite a lot of looking up in tables etc.)
◆ Finally you compare the measured altitude to the predicted altitude. This tells you how far away you are from the assumed position, and therefore enables you to draw a position line.

One position line does not give your position. You can get another one, and hence your position where they cross. This can be done:

◆ By simultaneously taking a sight on another body, or
◆ By sighting the sun a few hours later, when it has moved

In the latter case (known as the sun-run-sun procedure) you have to transfer the first position line by the distance run between the sights, as you do with a running fix.

The noon, or meridian passage, sight (see page 78) is a much simpler calculation, but it can only be done at one time in the day and only gives your latitude.

✳ Tip
A single position line can nevertheless be useful. It doesn't tell you where you are, but as someone once put it: 'It tells you where you ain't.' It can, for example, tell you that you are reasonably clear of dangers.

Declination, GHA and LHA

The Nautical Almanac gives the positions (as observed from the earth) of the sun, moon, planets and stars for every hour, of every day, of the year. From that, we can work out their positions for every second of the year.

It gives these positions in terms of two angles. These are declination and Greenwich hour angle (GHA). These are explained below using the sun as the example, but the moon, planets and stars work in exactly the same way.

Declination

Declination is the latitude of the place on the earth where the sun is directly overhead. Like latitude, it is measured in degrees and minutes north or south of the equator. Declination changes slowly and continuously.

Declination of the sun	
Solstice	
20/21 June	Just over 23°N
June–September	North declination decreases
Equinox	
22 September	0° (overhead at the equator)
September–December	South declination increases
Solstice	
21/22 December	Just over 23°S

Declination is tabulated for every hour of every day in *The Nautical Almanac*. You apply a small correction to get its value for the minute of the time of your sight.

Declination, GHA and LHA

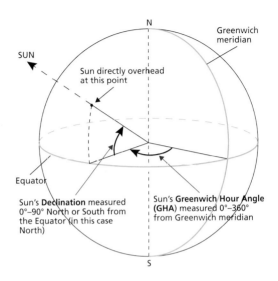

Fig 4.2 Declination and GHA.

Greenwich hour angle

The other angle, GHA, changes much more quickly. It is the angle that changes due to the earth's spin. When the sun's GHA is zero, it is noon at the Greenwich meridian. Every hour after that it increases by 15°, so that it goes full circle in 24 hours.

GHA is measured (in degrees and minutes) in a similar way to longitude, except that it goes from 0° to 360° in a westerly direction (whereas longitude is measured from 0° to 180° east or west). It is tabulated for every hour of every day, and you then have to apply quite a large correction to get the GHA for a particular minute and *second* of the time of your sight.

Local hour angle

Whereas GHA is measured from the Greenwich meridian, the local hour angle (LHA) is measured from your position or assumed position. To calculate LHA, simply adjust GHA by your longitude (subtract if you are west of Greenwich, or add if east).

Position line

It is helpful to understand how measuring the sun's altitude above the horizon can give a position line. Imagine the earth stationary (not spinning) at a particular time, with the sun fixed in one place. There is one point on the earth where the sun is vertically overhead. Here, it is at 90° to the horizon whichever way you measure it.

If you walk away from that point in a straight line (in any direction) you will get to a point where you have gone 1° round the earth. Now the angle of the sun to the horizon will be 89°. Carry on for a further 1° round the earth in the same direction, and the sun will be at 88° to the horizon. This would happen in whatever direction you walked.

So you can imagine a series of circles, centred on the point on the earth where the sun is vertically overhead. At any point on each of these circles the sun will be at the same angle to the horizon (altitude), say 88° for a particular circle. Thus a measurement of 88° means you are somewhere on that position circle (see Fig 4.3).

Now when the altitude is smaller, say 45°, the position circle you are standing on is very large – several thousand miles in diameter – so the small section you are interested in will approximate to a straight line.

Position line

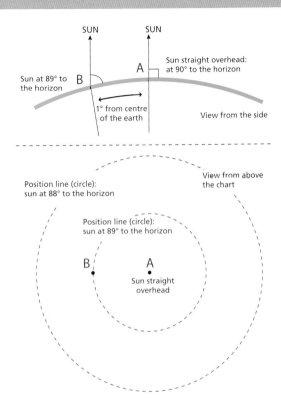

Fig 4.3 Position circles around the point where the sun is straight overhead.

Drawing a position line for your location

You can work out the altitude and azimuth of the sun at an assumed position close to your own position. Suppose that the altitude you work out is 44°, and suppose that you have measured the sun, and its altitude was 44° 30'. That means you are exactly 30' closer to where the sun

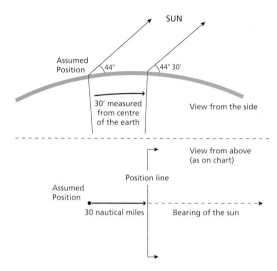

Fig 4.4 How the position line is drawn from the Assumed Position.

is directly overhead (see Fig 4.4). 30' on this great circle is 30NM. So you can draw a position line exactly 30NM from the assumed position, towards the sun.

The position line is part of a huge circle with the sun directly above the centre, so the line is drawn at right angles to the direction of the sun. The sight reduction has also given you the bearing of the sun at that point (its azimuth), so now you have all the information you need to draw the position line on the chart.

The noon (meridian passage) sight

At midday (not necessarily 1200 on your watch, see below) the sun is at its highest point in the sky, and is due south if you are in northern latitudes. Suppose the sun's declination at that moment is 10°N. If you were on the equator, the sun would not be exactly overhead. It would, in fact, be north of you, and would be 10° away from vertically overhead, so its altitude would be (90° − 10°) = 80°, to the north.

If you stood at 10°N the sun would be exactly overhead (90° to the horizon), and if you were at 20°N it would now be south of you, at 80° to the horizon. At 30°N it would be 70° to the horizon, and so on. So it is fairly simple to see the formula: **90° minus the altitude of the sun** is your angular distance from the point where the sun is directly overhead.

Fig 4.5 shows the case where both latitude and declination are north. If latitude and declination are the **same**, ie both north or both south, then the formula is:

latitude = 90° − altitude + declination.

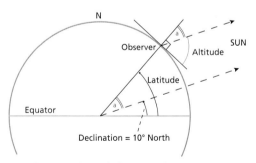

- ◆ The two angles marked **a** are equal.
- ◆ **a** is Latitude minus Declination (in this example)
- ◆ also: **a** = 90° − Altitude (measured by observer)
- ◆ So: 90° − Altitude = Latitude − Declination
- ◆ Hence: Latitude = 90° − Altitude + Declination

Fig 4.5 Meridian passage altitude for the sun.

If latitude and declination are **contrary**, ie one is north and the other south, then:

latitude = 90° – altitude – declination.

The measured altitude needs to be corrected in the same way as a normal sight (see page 90), and the declination is looked up in *The Nautical Almanac* for the day and hour of the observation (see page 92).

TIME OF MERIDIAN PASSAGE

◆ The sun crosses the Greenwich Meridian at anything between 11.44 GMT and 12.14 GMT, depending on the time of year. So meridian passage at Greenwich is 12.00 GMT plus or minus the equation of time, which is given in *The Nautical Almanac* for each day of the year.

◆ Adjust for your longitude. Meridian passage is earlier if you're east of Greenwich, later if you're west. For a longitude of D degrees M minutes, the time difference from Greenwich is: **4D minutes + 4M seconds.**

EXAMPLE: 17 October 2014, from *The Nautical Almanac*

Sun's meridian passage is **11h 45m**.

Equation of time (at 12h) is **14m 32s**.

So the exact meridian passage time at Greenwich is:

12h 00m 00s – 00h 14m 32s = **11h 45m 28s**.

At 32°N 11'W (near the Azores) meridian passage is:

11h 45m 28s + (4 x 32) minutes + (4 x 11) seconds =
11h 45m 28s + 02h 08m 44s = **13h 54m 12s**.

✳ Tip

If you don't know the precise time, take a series of sights and select the greatest altitude.

The sextant

The sextant

A sextant (or octant, which is similar) is an optical instrument for measuring the angle between two distant objects. The sextant gives the user two views, side by side, of two distant objects. When you line up the images, the instrument measures the angle between the lines of sight to the two objects.

◆ One line of sight is straight ahead (the red Line A in Fig 4.6).

◆ The other is along the green line B. This view is a reflection in the fixed horizon mirror (M1), back to the index mirror (M2), then out to the object.

◆ The angle between lines A and B is changed by rotating the index mirror M2, which is attached to the index arm.

◆ The scale, on the arc at the bottom of the instrument, is calibrated very accurately to read the angle between the two lines.

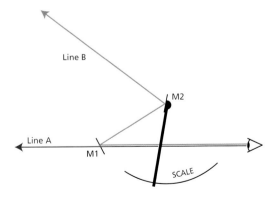

Fig 4.6 How a sextant works.

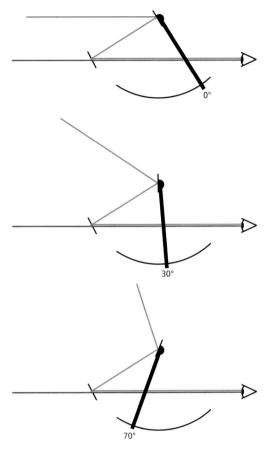

Fig 4.7 Here, the sextant is set to three different angles: zero (sight lines parallel), 30° and 70°.

The sextant

Fig 4.8 Parts of a typical yacht sextant:

A Telescope that the user sights through.

B Horizon mirror. Only half of this is mirror: the other half is plain glass, or open space so you can see past the mirror. This places the two views or images side by side. To the viewer they overlap slightly at the blurred edge between them.

C Index Mirror, which is fixed to the index arm.

D Index arm.

E Scale marked in degrees.

F Knob attached to a worm screw, so that when you turn it the arm moves slowly along the scale. (The worm can be disengaged with a lever, to allow free movement of the index arm.)

G Scale of minutes. A full rotation of F moves the arm by exactly one degree on the scale. The minutes scale shows the sub-divisions of a degree – 60 minutes for a full rotation of the knob, like a micrometer.

H Two sets of dark glass filters that can make bright objects (sun) safe to view through the telescope.

✳ Tip
Using the sextant is a skill that requires hands-on practice.

◆ It's a precision instrument, so be gentle with it.
◆ Pick it up by the frame, not the index arm or the mirrors.
◆ When not in use, keep it in its box.
◆ Be careful when looking through the telescope towards the sun. Use the shades provided.

How to use it

Start off by setting the scale to zero degrees and zero minutes. Then hold the instrument up to your eye and look through the telescope. You are looking at two images, side by side. If you twist the knob (F in Fig 4.8) back and forth, you should see one of the images moving up and down against the other.

The first thing you need to do is measure the index error. Looking at the horizon, twist the knob until the horizon line in the two images is exactly aligned. It should look like a continuous line with no 'step'. Then read the scale. The degrees scale should be zero, and the minutes will probably be a small number away from zero, in one direction (1, 2, 3 ... here the error is 'on' the scale) or the other (59, 58, 57 ... error 'off' the scale). Note the index error, and whether 'on' or 'off'.

To measure the angle between two objects, you move the index arm so that the two objects appear side by side when you look through the telescope. Line them up exactly by twisting the knob, and then you can read the angle from the degrees and minutes scales.

The sextant

* Tip

The object you use to measure index error must be distant, or the reading will be rubbish. Try it with something close and you'll see what I mean.

For astro navigation, the two objects in question are the sun (or moon, planet, star) and the horizon line. What you need is the least angle you can get with the horizon line. If you move the sextant away from vertical a bit, you will find that the sun 'swings' up off the horizon line as if it was on a pendulum (see Fig 4.9). So the technique is to tilt the sextant one way and then the other, and take the reading where the sun just grazes the horizon at the lowest point of its swing. This gets easier with practice. Start with the sun or moon, because it's a bit harder with a planet or star.

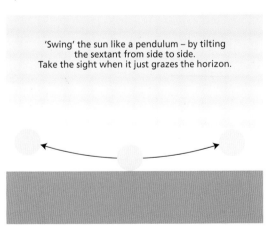

'Swing' the sun like a pendulum – by tilting the sextant from side to side.
Take the sight when it just grazes the horizon.

Fig 4.9 'Rocking' the sextant to take a sight on the Sun (lower limb).

✳ **Tip**

Quite often the difficult part is 'finding' the sun in the first place. One technique is to set the arm to zero, then tilt the sextant up until it points to the sun (watch your eyes, use both sets of shades). Then you bring the instrument slowly down to horizontal, simultaneously moving the index arm out to keep the sun in view. It may help to keep the other eye open while you're doing this. Once the instrument is horizontal you can do the fine adjustment and take the sight.

Adjustments

There are three errors that you can correct on the sextant, using adjustment screws on the back of the mirrors. In practice, you don't need to do this very often.

◆ **Perpendicularity** The index mirror needs to be perpendicular to the plane of the instrument. To check this, place the index arm roughly in the centre of the scale. Then, looking across the instrument from the opposite side to the scale, you should see the scale lined up with its reflection in the index mirror (see Fig 4.10).

◆ **Side error** Side error is the sideways separation of the two images. It's not critical for the accuracy of a sight; in fact, a small side error may be helpful to distinguish between identical images. Set the index to zero, and sight a distant object (preferably one with a clear vertical edge). Observe the separation of the two identical images by moving the sextant slightly from side to side.

The sextant

Fig 4.10 Perpendicularity. In this example it might need a very small adjustment.

✳ Tip

If you are at sea, with only the horizon to sight, hold the sextant on its side, then adjust to eliminate the vertical 'step' in the horizon between the two images.

◆ **Index error** Critical to the accuracy of the sight, it is normal practice to measure the index error each time you take a set of sights and adjust the sight accordingly (see page 83 for a description of how to measure it). If it is more than a few minutes, you can adjust it with the screw on the back of the fixed horizon mirror that rotates the mirror in the same sense that the index mirror rotates. Set the degrees and minutes scales to zero, sight on the horizon and adjust the mirror until there is no 'step' in the horizon.

Step-by-step instructions

The following instructions use a form. You can make up your own from the figures in the following pages, or download one from http://www.aztecsailing.co.uk.

The advantages of using a form are:

◆ It helps you to work methodically and make fewer stupid mistakes (eg copying numbers incorrectly).

◆ If you do get a rubbish answer, you (or someone else) can check back through the form and find out where you went wrong. There's no need to throw the sight away – just correct the fault and continue from there.

✳ Tip

When you're learning, it's very much less frustrating if you can check your work, find the fault and correct it, rather then starting again with another sight. You learn by seeing where you went wrong.

◆ Once you have done a few sights, you will find that the form guides you through the process, so you won't need to look at the instructions all the time.

The only mathematical skill you need is to add and subtract angles, which are expressed in degrees and minutes. A degree is divided into 60 minutes. So, for example:

14° 36′ + 10° 40′ = 25° 16′
68° 12′ − 22° 30.7′ = 45° 41.3′

With subtractions, it's a good idea to check the result with a quick 'add back'. So for the subtraction above:
45° 41.3′ + 22° 30.7′ = 68° 12′ checks that you got the answer right.

Step-by-step instructions

Take the sight

1. With the sextant, sight the horizon and measure the index error (see page 83). Note whether the error is 'on' or 'off' the scale. For example, a reading of 0° 4' is **4' on**; a reading of 55' is **5' off**. The index error correction is **+** if the error is **off**, and **–** if it is **on** the scale. Write this correction against IE in the right-hand column of the form.

✳ Tip

Remember to use the horizon for the index error measurement, because anything close to you (part of the boat, for example) will give a false reading.

2. Write on the form the date, body (sun) and circle U for upper or L for lower limb. Limb means the edge of the body concerned. You generally use the lower limb of the sun by sitting it on, not below, the horizon when taking the sight (see Fig 4.9).

3. Note the log reading so that you can use your sight to do a transferred position line or dead reckoning later.

4. Take four or five measurements of the sun's altitude. As you take each one, note the time to the nearest second.

✳ Tip

It helps if you have someone else looking at the watch and noting the readings. You call 'now' when you're happy with the sight. Let them write down the time, and then call out the sextant reading.

ASTRO NAVIGATION SIGHT REDUCTION FORM
using *Nautical Almanac Concise Sight Reduction Tables*

Date __12/5/08__   Body __Sun__   Limb U / Ⓛ   Log __3847.6__

Times	spot mean:		Angles	spot mean:	
10 19 12	+ / -	___	40 23	+ / -	___
10 19 56		___	40 29		___
10 20 47		___	40 36		___
10 21 04		___	40 41		___
10 21 34		___	40 43		___
	sum	___		sum	___
	sum/n	___		sum/n	___

Mean
(watch)

Mean

---

5. Enter the times and measured angles on the form.
6. If you see one reading that is obviously wrong, discard it (and its time). For example, if you are measuring the sun in the morning, each angle should be slightly greater than the last; if one is obviously out of sequence it is probably in error, so don't include it.
7. Average the times and altitudes. The easiest way to do this is by the 'spot mean' method: a) guess a round number mean value, then b) average the differences, plus and minus, either side of that guessed mean (see examples on the form below). Write down mean (watch) and mean (sextant).

ASTRO NAVIGATION SIGHT REDUCTION FORM
using *Nautical Almanac Concise Sight Reduction Tables*

Date __12/5/08__   Body __Sun__   Limb U / Ⓛ   Log __3847.6__

Times	spot mean:	10 20 00	Angles	spot mean:	40 35
10 19 12	+ / -	- 48	40 23	+ / -	- 12
10 19 56		- 4	40 29		- 6
10 20 47		+ 47	40 36		+ 1
10 21 04		+ 64	40 41		+ 6
10 21 34		+ 94	40 43		+ 8
	sum	+ 163		sum	- 3
	sum/n	+ 33		sum/n	- 1

Mean			Mean		
(watch)	10 20 33		(sextant)	40 34	
Zone adj	___		I E	+ 4	(4' OFF)
watch corr	___		Dip	___	
U T	___		App Alt	___	
			Alt corr 1	___	
HP	___		Alt corr 2	___	
Dec			U Limb corr	-30′	

Step-by-step instructions

✳ Tip

Get into the habit of looking at the result of your calculation and making sure that it is sensible, ie roughly what you expect – the common sense check.

Correct the time and altitude

8. In the left column of the form, put in the time zone adjustment (–1h if your watch is set to BST, for example). Put in the watch correction slow or fast. From those, adjust the mean watch time to get corrected Universal Time **UT**.

9. Go to the very first table of *The Nautical Almanac*: 'Altitude Correction Tables'. Look up **Dip** for the height of the sextant observation above sea level. (In this example, the observation is from 2m above sea level.) In the right column, apply IE and Dip to the mean sextant angle, to give **App Alt** (apparent altitude).

10. In the Altitude Correction tables, look up the altitude correction for the App Alt of the sun, and write it down as **Alt corr 1**.

11. Add Alt corr 1 to App Alt to get **True Alt H0**.

ASTRO NAVIGATION SIGHT REDUCTION FORM
using *Nautical Almanac Concise Sight Reduction Tables*

Date 12/5/08   Body   Sun   Limb U /Ⓛ   Log 3847.6

Times	spot mean:	10 20 00		Angles	spot mean:	40 35	
10 19 12	+/-	- 48		40 23	+/-	- 12	
10 19 56		- 4		40 29		- 6	
10 20 47		+ 47		40 36		+ 1	
10 21 04		+ 64		40 41		+ 6	
10 21 34		+ 94		40 43		+ 8	
	sum	+ 163			sum	- 3	
	sum/n	+ 33			sum/n	- 1	

Mean				Mean			
(watch)	10 20 33			(sextant)	40 34		
Zone adj	-1	(BST)		I E	+ 4	(4' OFF)	
watch corr	+23	(23s slow)		Dip			
U T	09 20 56			App Alt			
				Alt corr 1			
HP				Alt corr 2			
Dec (h)	N/S			U Limb corr		-30'	
d (m)				True Alt H₀			
Dec	N/S						

T REDUCTION FORM
e Sight Reduction Tables

A2 ALTITUDE CORRECTION TABLES 10°–90'—SU

Limb U /Ⓛ   Log 3847.6

Angles	spot mean:	40 35	
40 23	+/-	- 12	
40 29		- 6	
40 36		+ 1	
40 41		+ 6	
40 43		+ 8	
	sum	- 3	
	sum/n	- 1	

Mean		
(sextant)	40 34	
I E	+ 4	(4' OFF)
Dip	- 2.5	
App Alt	40 35.5	
Alt corr 1	+ 14.9	
Alt corr 2		
U Limb corr		-30'
True Alt H₀	40 50.4	

	OCT MAR SUN APR SEPT					DIP			
	App. Alt	Lower Limb	Upper Limb	App. Alt	Lower Limb	Upper Limb	Ht. of Eye	Corrⁿ	Ht. of Eye	Corrⁿ
							m		ft.	
	9 33	+10·8	-21·5	9 39	+10·6	-21·2	2·4	-2·8	8·0	-1·8
	9 45	+10·9	-21·4	9 50	+10·7	-21·1	2·6	-2·9	8·6	1·5
	9 56	+11·0	-21·3	10 02	+10·8	-21·0	2·8	-3·0	9·2	2·5
	10 08	+11·1	-21·2	10 14	+10·9	-20·9	3·0	-3·1	9·8	
	10 20	+11·2	-21·1	10 27	+11·0	-20·8	3·2		3·0	3·0
	10 33	+11·3	-21·0	10 40	+11·1	-20·7		-3·3		See table
	10 46	+11·4	-20·9	10 53	+11·2	-20·6	3·6	-3·4	11·2	
	11 00	+11·5	-20·8	11 08	+11·3	-20·5	3·8	-3·5	12·6	m
	11 15	+11·6	-20·7	11 22	+11·4	-20·4	4·0	-3·6	13·3	20 -7·9
	11 45	+11·7	-20·6	11 37	+11·5	-20·3	4·3	-3·7	14·1	22 8·3
				11 53			4·5		14·9	
	34 15	+14·9	-17·4	32 13	+14·7	-17·1				
	36 14	+15·0	-17·3	37 24		-17·0				
	38 34	+15·1	-17·2	40	+14·9	-16·9				
	41 06	+15·2	-17·1	42		-16·8				
	43 56	+15·3	-17·0	45 29	+15·1	-16·7				
	47 07	+15·4	-16·9	48 52						

Step-by-step instructions

Determine Dec and LHA

12. Back to the left-hand column. Leave **HP** blank – that's for moon only.

13. Beside **Dec**, write the UT hour in the brackets. Go to the 'Daily Pages' in *The Nautical Almanac*. Look up declination for the sun for the UT hour on the correct date. Note whether it is N or S by circling the appropriate letter, and make a mental note of whether the declination is increasing or reducing from one hour to the next.

14. Write down the value for **d** from the same day (it's at the bottom of the table: d is the amount declination changes by in one hour). Write down the UT minutes in the brackets.

15. Still in the Daily Pages, look up and write down the **GHA** for the sun for the same UT hour.

16. Go to the 'Increments and Corrections' table (towards the back of *The Nautical Almanac*), and find the page corresponding to the UT minutes. On this page, use the value of d to look up the correction to Dec.

17. Add or subtract the correction (according to whether declination is increasing or decreasing from one hour to the next) to get **Dec**. This is the best estimate of the declination at that UT time to the nearest minute.

18. On the same page of the Increments and Corrections table, look up the **increment** against the seconds of the UT time. Write this below the GHA from the Daily Pages.

19. Leave **v** blank – for moon and planets only.

20. Add the increment to the GHA from the Daily Pages, to give **GHA**. This is the best estimate of Greenwich Hour Angle at the UT time to the nearest second.

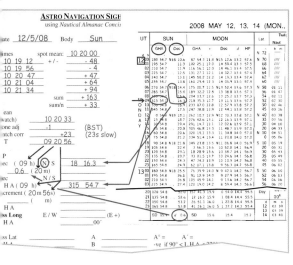

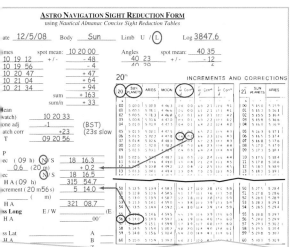

Step-by-step instructions

✳ Tip

There is a 'common sense' check for Dec and GHA. Once you have applied the increments and corrections to get Dec and GHA for the hour, minutes and seconds of UT, these should lie somewhere between the successive hourly values in the Daily Pages.

21. Choose, and write on the form, an assumed longitude **Ass Long** that is close to your estimated position, but comes to an exact number of degrees when you add it to, or subtract it from, GHA. Add ass long to GHA if it is an east longitude or subtract if west to get **LHA**. LHA should be a whole number of degrees, zero minutes.

22. Choose an assumed latitude **Ass Lat**, which is a round number of degrees close to your estimated position.

Sight reduction using tables

23. Copy Ass Lat and LHA to the next section on the form. Go to *The Nautical Almanac*'s 'Sight Reduction' table. Use Ass Lat and LHA to look up **A**, **B** and **Z_1** and write them on the form.

24. Write down **A°** (A rounded to the nearest degree, not necessarily rounded down) and **A'**, which is the minutes part of A.

25. Make B negative if LHA is between 90° and 270°. Make Z_1 the same sign as B.

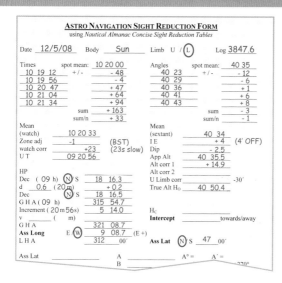

ASTRO NAVIGATION SIGHT REDUCTION FORM
using *Nautical Almanac Concise Sight Reduction Tables*

Date 12/5/08   Body Sun   Limb U /(L)   Log 3847.6

Times	spot mean:	10 20 00		Angles	spot mean:	40 35
10 19 12	+/-	- 48		40 23	+/-	- 12
10 19 56		- 4		40 29		- 6
10 20 47		+ 47		40 36		+ 1
10 21 04		+ 64		40 41		+ 6
10 21 34		+ 94		40 43		+ 8
	sum	+ 163			sum	- 3
	sum/n	+ 33			sum/n	- 1

Mean				Mean		
(watch)	10 20 33			(sextant)	40 34	
Zone adj	-1	(BST)		I E	+ 4	(4' OFF)
watch corr	+23	(23s slow)		Dip	- 2.5	
U T	09 20 56			App Alt	40 35.5	
				Alt corr 1	+ 14.9	

HP				Alt corr 2		
Dec (09 h) (N) S	18 16.3			U Limb corr		-30′
d 0.6 (20 m)	+ 0.2			True Alt H₀	40 50.4	
Dec (N) S	18 16.5					
GHA(09 h)	315 54.7			H꜀		
Increment (20 m 56 s)	5 14.0			**Intercept**		towards/away
v (m)						
GHA	321 08.7					
Ass Long E (W)	9 08.7	(E +)				
LHA	312 00′			**Ass Lat** (N) S	47 00′	

Ass Lat	____	A	____	A° =	A′ =
		B	____		270°

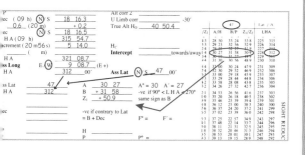

ec (09 h) (N) S	18 16.3		Alt corr 2		
0.6 (20 m)	+ 0.2		U Limb corr		-30′
ec (N) S	18 16.5		True Alt H₀	40 50.4	
HA(09 h)	315 54.7				
crement (20 m 56 s)	5 14.0		H꜀		
(m)			**Intercept**		towards/away
HA	321 08.7				
ss Long E (W)	9 08.7	(E +)			
HA	312 00′		**Ass Lat** (N) S	47 00′	

ss Lat	47	A	30 27	A° = 30 A′ = 27
HA	312	B	+ 31 58	-ve if 90° < L H A < 270°
		Zᵢ	+ 50.9	same sign as B
ec				-ve if contrary to Lat
				= B + Dec
		H		
		P		P° =

/Z₂	A/H	B/P	Zᵢ/Z₂	LHA
47				Lat / A
4 3	28 50	33 24	53 8	225 315
3 3	29 23	32 56	52 9	226 314
2 4	29 57	32 27	51 9	227 313
1 4	30 27	31 58	50 9	228 312
3 4	30 58	31 28	49 9	229 311
0 4	31 30	30 58	48 9	230 310
5 4	32 00	30 24	47 9	231 309
7 4	32 30	29 52	46 9	232 308
5 4	33 00	29 18	45 9	233 307
3 3	33 29	28 44	44 8	234 306
1 2	33 58	28 08	43 8	235 305
3 2	34 26	27 32	42 7	236 304
2 1	34 53	26 56	41 6	237 303
1 0	35 20	26 18	40 5	238 302
3 9	35 46	25 39	39 4	239 301
6 8	36 12	25 00	38 3	240 300
7 6	36 37	24 20	37 2	241 299
5 5	37 02	23 39	36 0	242 298
4 3	37 25	22 57	34 9	243 297
1 1	37 48	22 14	33 7	244 296
0 0	38 11	21 31	32 5	245 295
1 8	38 32	20 46	31 3	246 294
3 5	38 53	20 01	30 1	247 293
4 3	39 13	19 15	28 9	248 292

SIGHT REDUC

Step-by-step instructions

✳ Tip

It's a good idea to explicitly write + or – in front of a number when you're asked to 'make it' positive or negative. It shows you've completed that step in the process.

26. Copy B and Dec to the left-hand column, making Dec negative if it is contrary to Lat (ie if one is north and the other is south).

27. Add B and Dec (using their new + or – signs) to get **F**.

28. Write down **F°** (F rounded to the nearest degree) and **F′**, which is the minutes part of F.

29. Now copy A° and F° to the left-hand column and use them to look up in the Sight Reduction table again. This will give you **H**, **P** and **Z₂**. Write these down, and **P°** and **Z₂°**, which are P and Z_2 rounded to the nearest degree.

30. This second lookup in the Sight Reduction table needs two corrections, because you used A° and F° which were approximations to A and F.

Copy F′, P°, A′ and Z_2° to the left-hand column. Go to the Auxiliary table (last page of the Sight Reduction table).

Look up using F′ and P°, and this will give you **corr1**.

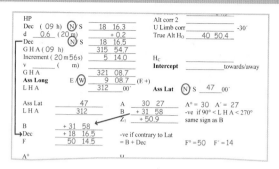

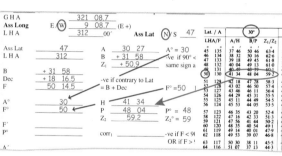

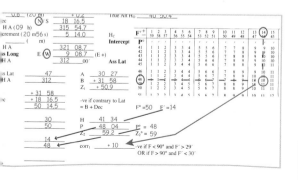

Step-by-step instructions

31. Also in the Auxiliary table, look up using A′ and Z_2°
and this will give you **corr2**.

32. Make corr1 negative if F<90° and F′>29′; or if F>90°
and F′<30′. Make corr2 negative if A′<30′.

33. You don't need to refer to *The Nautical Almanac*
again, so put it to one side.

34. Copy H, corr1 and corr2 to the left-hand column.
Add the positive or negative corrections to H to get
H_c, and finally make H_c negative if F is negative.

35. H_c is the calculated altitude for the sun at the
assumed position, so copy it up to the right-hand
side of the form just below True Alt H_o. Subtract the
smaller from the larger to get the **Intercept**, which
is going to be the distance (in degrees and minutes,
and hence nautical miles) of your position line from
the Assumed Position; towards or away from the
direction of the sun.

36. Circle **towards** if H_o is greater than H_c (meaning
you are closer to the sun), and **away** if H_o is less
than H_c.

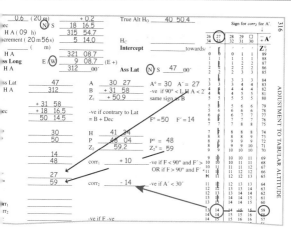

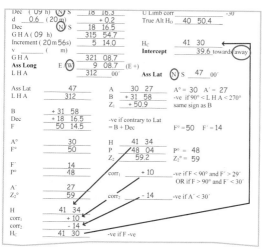

Step-by-step instructions

37. The final thing is to work out the azimuth. Copy Z_2 from above, and make it negative if F>90°.

38. On the next line, if F is negative, calculate and write down a new value for Z_2, which is 180°–Z_2 (otherwise leave blank).

39. Copy Z_1 from above, then add Z_1 and Z_2 together to get **Z**.

40. Finally, follow the rules on the form to calculate **Zn**, the azimuth:

In northern latitudes,
if **LHA>180° Zn = Z;** if **LHA<180° Zn = 360°–Z**.

In southern latitudes,
if **LHA>180° Zn = 180°–Z;** if **LHA<180° Zn=180°+Z**.

Draw the position line

41. You can do this on your ocean chart, or on special 'plotting sheets'. Mark the assumed position (using Ass Lat and Ass Long from the form).

42. Draw a line through the assumed position towards and away from the sun, using Zn from the form as the true bearing of the sun.

43. Measure off the intercept distance, either towards or away from the sun as indicated on the form (use the degrees and minutes of latitude on the side of the chart, close to the latitude of the assumed position).

44. At the point where you have measured off the Intercept, draw your position line at 90° to the first line.

45. Mark each end of the position line with arrows pointing towards the sun, and write the time and 'SUN' beside it.

Step-by-step instructions

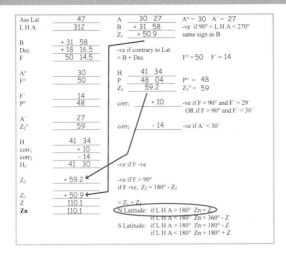

Ass Lat	47		A	30 27	$A° = 30$ $A' = 27$
L H A	312		B	+ 31 58	-ve if $90° <$ L H A $< 270°$
			Z_1	+ 50.9	same sign as B
B	+ 31 58				
Dec	+ 18 16.5		-ve if contrary to Lat		
F	50 14.5		= B + Dec		$F° = 50$ $F' = 14$
A°	30		H	41 34	
F°	50		P	48 04	$p° = 48$
			Z_2	59.2	$Z_2° = 59$
F'	14				
p°	48		corr$_1$	+ 10	-ve if $F < 90°$ and $F' > 29'$
					OR if $F > 90°$ and $F' < 30'$
A'	27				
$Z_2°$	59		corr$_2$	- 14	-ve if $A' < 30'$
H	41 34				
corr$_1$	+ 10				
corr$_2$	- 14				
H$_C$	41 30		-ve if F -ve		
Z_2	+ 59.2		-ve if $F > 90°$		
			if F -ve, $Z_2 = 180° - Z_2$		
Z_1	+ 50.9				
Z	110.1		$= Z_1 + Z_2$		
Zn	110.1		N Latitude: if L H A $> 180°$ Zn $= Z$		
			if L H A $< 180°$ Zn $= 360° - Z$		
			S Latitude: if L H A $> 180°$ Zn $= 180° - Z$		
			if L H A $< 180°$ Zn $= 180° + Z$		

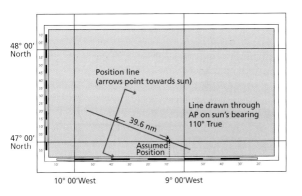

Sight reduction for other bodies

The process detailed above can be used for the moon, planets and stars, using the same form. There are a few differences, and this section outlines what they are. Apart from these differences, every other step is exactly the same as for the sun.

Moon

The moon is the most complex sight reduction. Additional corrections are needed because:

◆ The moon is close to the earth.
◆ Its movement (as seen from the earth) is more complex than the other bodies.

But from the navigation point of view the moon is extremely useful, because it is often visible during the day.

> ✳ **Tip**
> It's quite feasible to take a sun sight and a moon sight at the same time. If you do that you can get two position lines, and hence a fix.

DIFFERENCES IN THE PROCESS

1. You need to decide whether to use the moon's **upper** or **lower limb** (edge), ie whether to sit the moon on top of the horizon or underneath it. Mark this choice on the form.
   ◆ If you can see a crescent tipped 'on its back', the true edge of the moon can be seen at the bottom, and the top is just the end of the shadow – use the lower limb like the sun.

- ◆ If it looks like a crescent tipped forwards, the true edge can be seen at the top – use the upper limb (sit the moon under the horizon).

2. The moon has its own Altitude Correction table. Before you do the altitude corrections, write down **HP** from the Daily Pages. Its value is found next to GHA and Dec for the hour and day of the observation. Then turn to the Altitude Correction Tables – Moon, at the back of the almanac, and look up **Alt Corr 1** from the top half. Then look up **Alt corr 2** in the bottom half, opposite the value of HP, and in the same column as the first correction (under L for lower limb or U for upper). Both of these corrections are added. Subtract 30′ if you used the upper limb.

3. The moon has a value of d for every hour in the Daily Pages (unlike the sun which has one value covering three days). Apart from that, the use of d is the same.

4. When looking up the **increment** in the Increments and Corrections table, remember to use the column headed moon.

5. The moon also has a **v correction for the GHA**, which the sun does not. Simply take the value of v for the hour (it is next to GHA) and look in the Increments and Corrections table in exactly the same way as d. Then add this extra correction, as well as the increment, to get GHA.

From then on the process is exactly the same as for the sun.

Sight reduction for other bodies

Planets

You can take sights of Venus, Mars, Jupiter and Saturn, which are sometimes extremely bright in the evening or morning sky. *The Nautical Almanac* contains information that helps you to identify them.

✳ Tip

With both planets and stars, particularly at dusk, take the sight first and worry about identifying the object afterwards. As it gets darker it becomes easier to identify the planet or star, using the star charts, planet notes and tables in *The Nautical Almanac*.

So if you see a bright object in the evening sky, go ahead and take a sight on it while you can still see the horizon clearly. You can work out which planet it is after doing the sight, before you do the sight reduction.

If you get a wildly inaccurate result (a very large intercept) then you may have identified the object incorrectly. Don't repeat the sight. Use the same sight data on a new form, and redo the sight reduction for the correctly identified body.

DIFFERENCES IN THE PROCESS

1. Altitude correction uses the same table as the sun, at the front of *The Nautical Almanac*, but remember to look up **Alt corr 1** under 'stars and planets' rather than sun. Venus and Mars have an additional date-dependent correction listed in the same table, which can be written down as Alt corr 2.

2. Like the moon, the planets have a v correction for GHA. The values of v and d are given for each of the planets in the Daily Tables. Note that v is sometimes negative (for Venus only).

Apart from these two points, the process is identical to the sun.

Stars

The process is simpler for the stars, but they are harder to identify and sight against the horizon. But at dusk and dawn you have the opportunity to take sights of several stars at the same time, and this enables you to draw several position lines and become much more certain of your position fix.

DIFFERENCES IN THE PROCESS

1. Altitude correction is the same as the sun, but using the stars and planets section of the table.
2. Look up Dec for the star concerned in the Daily Pages. Dec changes slowly for stars, so don't worry about the hour of day, or about d.
3. Look up GHA for the hour for Aries in the Daily Pages. Use the increment for Aries. Instead of v, write down the **SHA** of the star, and add these three angles together to get GHA for the star. (If the total goes over 360°, just subtract 360). SHA is the sidereal hour angle, and it is used to give the GHA positions of all the stars in relation to a single reference point, Aries.

The rest is exactly the same as the sun.

Checking the compass

One of the products of the sight reduction procedure described above is Zn, the azimuth, or true bearing, of the sun, moon, planet or stars at the time of the sight. You can use this information to check the compass.

The simplest method is:

1. Maintaining a course reasonably close to your desired passage course, head directly towards an identified celestial body. Note the exact compass reading and the time. (You do not need to take a sight with the sextant.)
2. Using this time, work through the time correction and the sight reduction process above (ignoring anything to do with measured altitudes) to get Zn.
3. Zn is the yacht's true heading at the time of the observation. Apply the local magnetic variation (from the chart) and you have the yacht's actual magnetic heading. The difference between that and the compass reading is the deviation on that course. You may use this to correct the compass course you steer.

The yacht

Long-distance ocean sailing places different requirements on a yacht than coastal sailing close to home base. However benign your planned route, it's necessary to be prepared for severe conditions, possibly for long periods. Quite simply, your yacht must be seaworthy enough to get you through the worst weather you are going to encounter; you cannot run for shelter on a long passage. This puts a premium on:

◆ Stability
◆ Seaworthiness and sailing capability in heavy weather
◆ Robustness of the yacht's structure, including: rigging, hull fittings, deck fittings, keel and rudder

For more ambitious and adventurous cruising, eg in high northern latitudes or the Southern Ocean, you may need to consider a yacht that has been specifically designed and constructed for that purpose.

There are many choices, and it is wise to seek good advice. For the purposes of this section it is assumed that you have already selected and/or acquired a yacht suitable for the task you have in mind, in terms of the 'basics' (size, design, construction, and stability); and that it is in good condition.

✳ Tip

A yacht surveyor can advise you on the condition of the yacht, and whether equipment is correctly installed. For example, floorboards and any heavy items such as batteries should be secure, cupboard fastenings adequate, and a properly installed cooker should not be able to break out of its gimbals in a knock-down.

Sails

Beyond the choice of yacht, most yachts (and certainly most new production yachts) are, in the first instance, equipped for relatively short-range and short-term voyages. Before you embark on a long-distance voyage you will need extra equipment, and there are a number of areas where choices exist and decisions need to be made.

Communication and **Safety/Emergency** are covered in separate sections – see pages 131 and 161 respectively.

Sails

In addition to the yacht's normal suit of sails, it is wise to carry spare sails and material for repairs, eg:

◆ Sheets/strips/rolls of sail cloth (can have adhesive backing)
◆ Adhesive sail tape
◆ Needles
◆ Sail repair sewing twine
◆ A 'palm' for sewing

Additional sails may include:

◆ A special sail for light airs, such as a ghoster or cruising chute
◆ A storm jib
◆ A storm trysail

If you have a roller furling headsail – which is most cruisers' preference these days – it is also worth considering an additional forestay that can be rigged when required. This removable inner forestay has two advantages:

◆ It can be used to rig a second headsail for prolonged downwind sailing.

◆ If you need to set a storm jib, it will not be necessary to completely unfurl and drop the large headsail (which will probably have been almost completely rolled away in the stronger winds).

It may also be worth considering an extra track on the mast for the storm trysail, so that you don't have to remove the mainsail.

Downwind rig

Some of the most popular routes involve a substantial amount of sailing in favourable trade winds, and if this is the case it is worth considering a special downwind rig consisting of two headsails. This sail plan works well with self-steering, because the centre of force is well forward and symmetrical about the centre line of the yacht. It also saves chafe on the mainsail against the spreaders, prevents the headsail being masked by the main and flapping, and avoids any risk of gybing the main. Best of all it requires very little intervention by the crew, apart from adjustments for wind strength, or if you need to gybe.

✳ Tip

In stark contrast to coastal sailing and racing, with trade wind sailing it is quite surprising how seldom you need to adjust the sails. I read about one yacht where the possibility of gybing that day was discussed at breakfast, and the conclusion was to discuss it again the next day.

Downwind rig

Racers may prefer the more dashing option of flying a spinnaker, but when crossing an ocean relatively short-handed, most cruisers prefer this low-maintenance alternative.

It's possible to get specially made 'double headsails' for this arrangement, such that a pair of sails is rigged on a single forestay with roller furling. The sails are of equal size as you unfurl, and a hinged double pole is used to hold the two clews to port and starboard.

The alternative, requiring the extra forestay but no other special gear, is to set the roller-furling headsail, poled out on the more windward side with the spinnaker pole; and hoist a second sail, with hanks, on the other forestay. This second sail can be poled out on

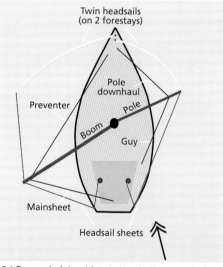

Fig 5.1 Downwind rig with twin headsails, using the boom and spinnaker pole.

the leeward side using the boom (with the mainsail flaked onto it and covered) by running the sheet through a block at the end of the boom (see Fig 5.1). This arrangement is not exactly symmetrical and favours a broad reach with the wind on the side of the spinnaker pole, but it can usually handle a range of wind directions before you have to gybe the whole thing.

✻ Tip
Remember to protect against chafe (of sails and lines), particularly on a prolonged downwind passage. This can be done with protective rags, or by slightly altering the position of the lines/sails from time to time.

Self-steering
For all but the hardiest crews, self-steering is an absolute necessity. There are two possible ways to achieve it:

◆ Wind vane self-steering
◆ Electronic autopilot

The respective pros and cons are summarised below, but ultimately the choice comes down to how you see your boat.

◆ For a simple, reliable wind-powered solution, in tune with sailing, go for the wind vane.
◆ For a high power-consumption boat with substantial use of electronics and motoring, choose a quality autopilot with good reliability.

Wind vane
This is a mechanical device that (depending on the design) steers either with the yacht's own rudder or with its own separate rudder. Once the yacht is sailing

Fig 5.2 Wind vane in action.

on the desired course, a vane is adjusted to the direction of the wind. If the yacht starts to go off course relative to the wind, the mechanism will steer it back again. There are several designs available, and you need to select one that is suitable for your yacht.

Although relatively heavy and bulky (and expensive), wind vanes are reliable and consume no power. They steer relative to the wind, so if the wind direction changes the yacht's course does too. This is beneficial in the open ocean, because the point of sail remains constant (there is, for example, little chance that the yacht will gybe). Close to shore or other craft, however, the course will need to be carefully monitored. They cannot be used when motoring in light winds.

Autopilot

There are a number of designs of electronic autopilot. They have a direction sensor (such as a fluxgate compass) and a small motor to steer using the yacht's rudder. Some designs can steer to the wind as an alternative; they obtain wind direction from a small wind sensor or from the yacht's other systems.

These devices are relatively inexpensive, but it's probably fair to say that the cheaper devices are aimed at the 'weekend sailing' market, and fall short of the reliability needed for long-distance cruising. They also consume power, which is a disadvantage for long passages.

Steering to a compass course, you need to watch the sail trim if the wind changes, and there is the possibility of an inadvertent gybe. On the other hand, autopilots are well suited to motoring, when power isn't a problem.

Berthing and anchoring

Away from home waters you may need to deal with rather more rugged berthing situations than you are used to. Consider carrying:

◆ A fender board, useful for berthing on rough harbour walls
◆ Additional long warps, eg for shore lines

Some of the places you might want to visit may have few harbours and no marinas, and anchoring will become a way of life so it's worth being self-reliant when it comes to ground tackle. Even in tropical waters, you can expect to encounter occasional strong winds and unpleasant conditions in supposedly 'sheltered' anchorages.

Carry a second anchor, if anything larger than your ordinary bower anchor. Some extra chain is helpful but not too much since you may need to take the gear out in the tender to set the second anchor when the wind gets up. This anchor can also be used from the stern if conditions dictate, eg to prevent the yacht from swinging with the tide.

You will need a good tender and outboard, and some arrangement to lock them up when you leave them.

Electrical power
The power equation

Most yachts depend on 12-volt (or 24-volt) DC electrical power to a greater or lesser extent, and your approach to generating and using electrical power is an important part of yacht preparation.

The power equation is as follows: **amp-hours (AH) used in a 24 hour period = AH generated in a 24-hour period.**

This doesn't matter very much on short trips, because any excess usage is made up by a small amount of motoring and/or shore power at the end. But for a longer trip you need to do some sums at the planning stage, and ideally monitor it at sea. You must always be able to generate more electrical power than you use.

There are, essentially, two routes to go down:

◆ Low power, and minimum reliance on power
◆ High power, with plenty of back-up for generating it

✳ Tip

To run a laptop computer off the 12V supply you can buy a device that supplies it at a slightly higher voltage than the battery (ie the same voltage that the laptop gets from its charger). This is more efficient than using an inverter (which produces mains voltage from the battery).

Low power route

If you opt for low reliance on power, then you typically choose:

◆ Wind vane self-steering
◆ Not to rely on refrigeration to keep food
◆ Not to rely on a watermaker – carry the water you need
◆ Simple instruments, eg a hand-held GPS
◆ Not to use 'domestic' kit for cooking or entertainment at sea (such as a microwave or TV)
◆ Masthead tricolour at night and careful use of cabin lights

Your power usage can be reduced to:

◆ Basic instruments, such as the log
◆ Lights (consider installing LEDs for further saving)
◆ Occasional use of radio

You will still have to generate power, but not very much, and this gives more flexibility and choice in how to do it. The main options are:

◆ Solar cells
◆ Wind power
◆ Water power (a turbine towed or deployed in the water)

The above should suffice, without the need to use the yacht's engine on a daily basis.

High power route

If you decide to be heavily reliant on power (particularly if you are depending on it for your food and water needs), you will need beefier kit – including spares and fall-backs – to generate it. This may include a generator,

Electrical power

✳ Tip
If you do run the engine at sea, remember to put it in gear. Running under load it is more likely to generate enough exhaust gases to expel any water that might enter the exhaust vent in rough conditions.

which gives you the added luxury of 240V power while it's running.

This is the way larger yachts tend to be set up. You get more luxury, but this comes not only at the price of buying the kit, but also understanding how to identify faults, carrying spares and knowing what to do when it goes wrong (note the use of 'when', rather than 'if').

With the high power route you can afford more luxury, and you can choose:

◆ Electric/electronic autopilot
◆ Refrigerated/frozen food and drink
◆ Watermaker
◆ Routine use of sophisticated navigation and communication equipment

This list can, of course, extend indefinitely, and include air-conditioning, heating, microwave oven, washing machine and other domestic appliances.

✳ Tip
Don't try to repair a 240V generator unless you know exactly what you're doing and take the necessary precautions. A mains electric shock, particularly when you are in contact with salt water, could be fatal.

Power equation example

This example was calculated for extended duration at sea, for a 55ft yacht.

Power usage (24-hour estimates)	
General usage of power at sea including lighting, use of fridge/freezer, tricolour light, autopilot, instruments, and very light use of SSB radio and radar	150AH
Calculated from the average length of time needed to fully recharge the batteries – about 3 hours with a 50A battery charger	
Watermaker, generating 40L per day, running for just over 3 hours	25AH
Calculated using manufacturer's figures	
TOTAL with contingency	**up to 200AH**

Power generation (three options, without running main engine at sea)	
DuoGen wind/water generator (wind 12.5–18kts, or water 4.8–6.8kts; unit can generate approx 5–10A)	120–240AH (depends on wind speed)
Taken from manufacturer's figures	
Solar cells, 2m² installed	66AH (depends on sun)
4kVA generator, runs at approx 25% of full load to drive 50A battery charger	4 hours for 200AH, uses 1.6L fuel
Calculated using manufacturer's figures	

Batteries

The example illustrates how the power equation impinges on other issues:

◆ How you use power for domestic purposes, including food preservation – and thus what type of food you carry.
◆ How much water you plan to make, or need to carry (see page 146).
◆ How much fuel you carry to run the generator.

✳ Tip

You can buy devices that make the engine alternator work harder in order to charge a domestic battery bank in a shorter time. If you decide on one of these, make sure you also upgrade the alternator (and carry a spare), because the regular alternator will not be adequate for the heavier workload.

Batteries

✳ Tip

Domestic batteries should be the 'deep cycle' type which are intended to be discharged by a substantial amount on a regular basis (as opposed to automotive batteries whose life will be shortened by this kind of use).

You need sufficient capacity in your 'domestic' battery bank to supply the electrical needs of the yacht until the batteries are recharged. The sensible approach is to assume a 24-hour charge/use cycle, remembering that you can significantly reduce battery life if you regularly discharge by more than 50%. On that basis you need a battery capacity of at least double the anticipated 24-hour usage.

In the example above you need at least 400AH. A greater capacity will be less harsh on the batteries, and will act as a reserve if for any reason you don't recharge fully each day.

A battery monitor, showing amps charging/discharging and remaining battery capacity, is extremely helpful. You can:

◆ Monitor the usage/generation during the passage – eg are the solar cells meeting the current demand?
◆ See how the estimates are working out.
◆ Make informed decisions about when to recharge.

Water making/storage

The amount of water needed on long passages is discussed on page 146: this section considers how you may plan to make it or carry it. If you decide to install a water maker, you need to consider the power implications. You also need to consider the reliability of the water maker itself, and carry spares to fix it if it goes wrong, such as:

◆ Spare membrane
◆ Filters
◆ Parts for the pump/plumbing

✷ Tip

The collapsible variety of water container sold for camping is useful as they don't take up too much space when empty (ie on the rest of your trip when you don't need them, but do need the space).

If you decide against a water maker, you need to be able to store all the water you will require for the longer passages. The 'normal' fresh water tank will probably

*Fig 5.3
Water maker
installation.*

be insufficient. Portable containers are a good option and can be preferable to large tanks, because you can actually see the water, and take it with you if you have to abandon to the liferaft. If a large tank splits or becomes contaminated, you lose all the water in it.

Consider carrying a small, hand-operated water maker for emergencies.

Pre-trip checks, spares and tools

Long-distance sailing is a spur to becoming more self-sufficient, and learning how to look after various parts of your yacht, be it the engine, the electrics or the rig. Although it is possible to get 'experts' to come and fix things, they may not be readily available, they may be expensive and speak a foreign language, and they certainly aren't on call at sea.

Most skippers find they are happy to fix and maintain some things, but others are a 'black art'. You might be quite happy stripping a winch, but quail at the sight of the bundle of wires behind the switch panel. It is extremely helpful to get a friendly expert to:

◆ Look over any areas that you're not sure about.
◆ Check the state of the equipment.
◆ Show you any potential problem areas.
◆ Advise you what spares and tools to carry, and how to identify and fix faults.

You could take this approach with:

◆ The rig
◆ Electrical systems and wiring
◆ The engine

Reference books and training courses are also available in either 'general' yacht maintenance or specific areas such as electrics and diesel engines.

✴ Tip
Some sailing schools offer weekend general yacht maintenance courses, and in some cases – particularly if you arrange a course for a group of you – they may be willing to do the course on your own yacht. This is ideal, even if (or perhaps especially if) the instructor keeps finding deficiencies in your yacht.

Most yachts end up with quite a substantial collection of tools, and an extensive collection of 'bits' and materials, be they wires, connectors, different kinds of sticky tape, shackles, screws, nut and bolts.

As a general rule, there are some things that you can expect to find almost anywhere in the world, such as engine oil, or indeed a mechanic who understands diesel engines. Then there are others that will be very difficult to source, such as the specific oil filter or gasket you need for your engine. This logic can guide your preparation.

Spare parts to consider

- ◆ Alternator
- ◆ Battery charger
- ◆ Drive belts
- ◆ Filters
- ◆ Gaskets
- ◆ Impellers
- ◆ Bulbs
- ◆ Fuses
- ◆ Batteries
- ◆ Blocks
- ◆ Jammers
- ◆ Winch components

✴ Tip

Very often yachts help each other in far-flung locations – or even at sea. You can trade expertise and tools, particularly if you stay in touch on radio nets.

Although we all want to avoid rough weather, it is a good idea for yacht skippers to learn how to manage their yachts in increasingly severe conditions. This is not always easy – there will always be people who warn you that you are irresponsible if you take a yacht and crew out in what they consider to be unsuitable weather. But do it in stages – possibly with a more experienced skipper on board to advise – and you will gain important knowledge about sea conditions, how your yacht behaves in strong wind and larger waves, and how to live on board in rough conditions.

You may discover necessary modifications to the yacht (extra hand-holds for example), or indeed that the yacht simply isn't suitable for heavy conditions. You will certainly gain in knowledge and confidence.

✴ Tip

When you go out in conditions that are worse than you are used to, prepare the yacht and crew thoroughly, and make sure you have 'options' – eg an easy run back into shelter if you want to pull out.

Check and secure everything on decks and below, and use harnesses and life lines for the crew.

Wind

The most immediate effect of strong wind is that it makes the yacht difficult to handle under sail, so it's highly instructive to practise sailing in gale force winds in sheltered water. Learn how the yacht performs, into the wind and running, with storm sails. You may discover that you need a deeper reef in your mainsail.

Waves

Waves can become very large and still not pose a threat to the yacht in deep water. The boat simply rises up over them, like a small hill. The problem arises when the waves break, and the yacht is most vulnerable when it is beam-on to a breaking wave.

◆ In medium to strong winds (eg force 7) in the open ocean, it is the crests that break. This can be uncomfortable if your yacht gets caught by a bad wave, but these conditions are unlikely to knock down or roll a reasonably stable boat.

◆ In stronger winds the crest breaks become more frequent and violent, and the yacht may require active steering through the breaks.

◆ In shallow water or bad overfalls, the break is far more serious, and a 'total' break can roll a large yacht. For this reason the best option in bad conditions is to stay well away from the coast in deep water; do not attempt a tricky harbour or river entrance, especially with a shallow bar.

Practise sailing up-wind into the large steep waves that are typical in coastal waters, in the aftermath of a gale. If you find that the waves frequently stop the yacht, you may need more sail, to give the yacht more power.

Motoring into steep waves can also be a problem: when the yacht pitches steeply over a big wave, the propeller can come out of the water which causes cavitation. Surrounded by bubbles, it loses all power to propel the yacht until it gets rid of the air, generally in about 10 seconds (you can hear the air swirling round the propeller). Motor sailing, slightly off the wind with a deeply reefed mainsail, is far *more* effective in these circumstances.

In the scale of windy/stormy conditions, there comes a point when your main consideration is survival, and you need to adapt your tactics to that end. It's perfectly feasible, even with ocean sailing, to avoid that situation, but it is necessary to have in mind options for what you would do in such circumstances, and equip the yacht accordingly.

Heavy weather on passage

You can minimise the risk of encountering bad conditions by making passages at the right time of year. This is part of route planning (see page 43). However it is not feasible to predict a 'weather window' for a longer passage, so there is always a risk that conditions will deteriorate.

Warning

To get advanced warning of bad weather, monitor:

◆ Weather forecasts
◆ Reports from other yachts
◆ Barometer
◆ Cloud formations and squalls within sight

Weather forecasts can cover quite a large area of sea (and may not be fully accurate), so local signs are very important.

Preparation

If you expect a prolonged period of bad weather, prepare early.

SECURE THE BOAT

◆ Remove and stow below any items that are normally stowed on deck.

Heavy weather on passage

- Check that any others (like liferafts) are securely lashed.
- Check hatches and lockers.
- Secure the washboard in place in the companion-way.
- Below, check that everything is securely stowed and lashed, particularly heavy objects.

PREPARE THE CREW

Crew members may be nervous at the prospect of heavy weather, and early, calm preparation will help.

- Use tablets (and other remedies) to prevent seasickness.
- Make sure everyone has warm, dry clothing stowed within easy reach.
- Prepare food that can easily be heated and eaten when things get bad.
- Encourage everyone to eat well and get plenty of sleep in advance of the bad weather.
- Make sure the watch pattern matches the stronger and weaker crew.
- Brief the crew about clipping on in the cockpit, and precautions moving around when it gets rough (hold on and/or crawl).

✳ Tip

As skipper, try to remain confident (or at least look as if you are). This will help to keep the crew's spirits up.

Heavy weather tactics

As conditions deteriorate, you need to judge when different tactics may be needed for the safety of the yacht. Your actions at this stage depend on number/strength of crew, on the way the yacht is responding to the conditions, and how extreme the conditions are likely to become.

Before the trip, you should plan what you would do (or attempt to do) in 'survival' conditions. It is well worth reading other sailors' accounts of what they did, studying their advice, and trying out tactics with your own yacht and crew.

◆ Stay away from shallow water, particularly a lee shore. Ideally you need to be able to weather the storm by choosing a heading that suits the wind and sea conditions, without having to worry about other dangers.

◆ If you have a full crew, you can keep the boat under control and moving (with a small amount of sail), steering through the waves by hand. If you are relatively short-handed, steering by hand may become too tiring (and self-steering may not work well), so different tactics will be needed.

◆ The most dangerous situation is to take a bad breaking wave on the beam. Sailing up-wind (say, about 60° to the wind) enables you to steer up into a break, and gives you control.

✳ Tip

Wind-vane self-steering works well into the wind, so sailing slowly up-wind may be an alternative to heaving to.

Heavy weather tactics

◆ Running before the wind is obviously attractive if that's where you want to go. It reduces the apparent wind (a good short-term measure), but in extreme conditions you may need to slow the boat down so that you don't lose control or surf dangerously down the waves. You can drag a large loop of warp, or drogues: 'series' drogues (a number of drogues on a long line) are particularly effective.

◆ Heaving to is also an option. Contrary to what many believe, this can be done without a backed head-sail: most yachts can successfully heave to under deeply reefed main, or under a sail set further aft. If you do this the bows will turn more to windward (and into the breaking waves) than they would otherwise.

Heaving to

To heave to (reefed mainsail only):

◆ Sheet the main hard in.
◆ Point the yacht into the wind until it loses all headway.
◆ Bows will 'fall off' on one or other tack.
◆ Put the helm hard over, as if to tack back through the wind, and secure it in that position.

The Pardeys (in their excellent book *Storm Tactics*) claim that the 'slick' of disturbed water, extending up-wind from a hove-to yacht, disrupts breaking waves, effectively protecting the boat.

◆ A sea anchor seems to be a mixed blessing. It will bring the bows to windward, and slow your downwind drift (particularly desirable if you do have a lee shore). Against this, the forces are huge (on the rode, where you secure to the yacht, and on the rudder if the yacht is thrown backwards). A large downwards force on the bows may be unhelpful. In theory a bridle can be rigged so that the yacht lies at an angle to the wind; however in my experience the yacht can persist in tacking through the wind, with the bridle going under the boat.

◆ Keep a watch system going, and send 'spare' crew below as conditions deteriorate: there is no point in everyone getting exhausted at the same time. You can place one or more crew on 'hot stand-by': lying down in a saloon berth in full waterproofs, so that they are instantly available in an emergency. If you are hove-to, the on-watch crew can shelter below for much of the time.

✳ Tip
A Perspex washboard is useful, because you can keep an eye on the helmsman while sheltering below.

The biggest worry is losing someone overboard, in conditions where it would be almost impossible to recover them.

◆ NEVER let anyone into the cockpit without being clipped on first.
◆ Clip onto the high side (particularly the helmsman): the roll of a yacht on a breaking wave could throw someone out of the cockpit.
◆ Use spare lines to stay clipped on when moving around.
◆ Waves taken onto the deck or into the cockpit are particularly dangerous.

Heavy weather tactics

The **skipper** needs to keep making and implementing decisions, and can only do this if they look after themselves. The three main dangers are:

◆ Lack of rest
◆ Lack of food sustenance – your metabolism is what keeps your brain functioning
◆ Discomfort, eg from cold wet clothing or needing to use the heads

You can put up with *one* of these for a while (you may have to), but if two or more 'get you' your brain and body function will be seriously impaired, and eventually you will just give up.

So if you're tired, make sure you go below and get something to eat; if you are wet, uncomfortable and irritable there is no reason you can't eat, rest, or use the heads. Don't get lethargic or put off going below 'because you might feel sick'.

At the end of a strong blow, or when the front goes through, the wind can drop very suddenly. However the waves will still be just as large, and can become more confused and dangerous. At this stage it is even more important to keep the yacht under control, but beware of increasing sail too quickly – the wind can get up again, possibly from a different direction, just as suddenly.

✳ Tip
If this happens, put the motor on for a while. This quickly enables you to steer, to control the yacht, and you can see what the wind does next before increasing sail.

Communication options

Each form of communication has different benefits and limitations. The best advice is to think carefully about what your requirements are before spending a lot of money on sophisticated equipment that you won't use very much.

For example, a 3G smartphone may provide everything you need when you are cruising in coastal waters. If you only plan to be on ocean passage for relatively short periods, you may be able to do without access to email and internet during that time.

The table below gives an overview of options that are described in the following pages.

Overview of communication options		
Purpose	**Coastal**	**Ocean**
Talking to other vessels	◆ Line of sight: marine ◆ Long range and 'nets'	◆ VHF Radio ◆ HF radio
Keeping in touch with friends/ family at home: general internet use	◆ Mobile phone (voice) ◆ 3G/smartphones (voice, email, blog etc)	◆ HF radio via coast radio station (or HAM amateur) ◆ Satellite telephone ◆ Email/internet access via satellite
Getting weather information	◆ Regional VHF weather services ◆ 3G/smartphones internet access	◆ HF radio spoken weather/routing and national services ◆ HF radio weather fax ◆ Internet access via satellite ◆ Inmarsat C
Safety, assistance and rescue	◆ VHF to regional coast-guard ◆ EPIRB	◆ HF radio via coast radio station for assistance (eg medical) ◆ Inmarsat C (position reporting, text assistance and distress alert) ◆ Satellite telephone ◆ EPIRB

Radio

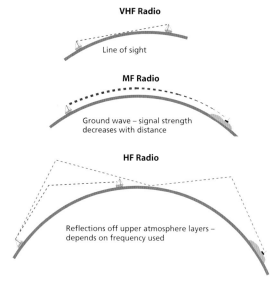

VHF Radio

Line of sight

MF Radio

Ground wave – signal strength
decreases with distance

HF Radio

Reflections off upper atmosphere layers –
depends on frequency used

Fig 7.1 Propagation of VHF, MF and HF radio waves.

✳ Tip

VHF use is more tightly regulated in some countries
than others. In European waters the coastguard
regularly reprimands people for infringing radio
telephony regulations. In Caribbean harbours,
anchored yachts chat happily to unlicensed shore
stations such as bars. Yachts and ships in mid
ocean regularly use Channel 16 for the whole
conversation, because no one else is in range.

VHF

Marine VHF is an ideal short-range solution, and is fitted on most yachts. It works if the antennae of the transmitting and receiving radios are in line of sight of one another (or shielded by only minor obstructions). That means that two vessels can communicate up to about 5NM from one another, and you can contact shore stations (eg coastguard) about 15–20NM away.

AIF is also VHF technology, and is useful for collision avoidance: particularly in busy shipping areas and poor visibility.

Although it is possible to patch through to the telephone system via coast radio stations, this is rarely used nowadays and has been largely superseded by the use of mobile phones.

Note that the frequencies associated with the radio channels (1–28, 60–88) differ slightly in different parts of the world. Most radio sets are able to switch between, say, 'USA' and 'International' to obtain the correct frequencies for the area.

Single sideband

Marine single sideband (SSB) radio operates in the frequency range of MF (300KHz–3MHz) and HF (3MHz–30MHz). Within these bands certain frequency ranges, using upper sideband, are allocated for use by 'maritime mobile' operators (ie us). 'Single sideband' refers to a type of radio transmission in which only part of the amplitude-modulated signal – the bit that carries the useful information, be it voice or data – is transmitted, requiring less transmitter power.

Understanding and using SSB is more complex than VHF. You need to go on a course (about five days) to learn how this radio operates, and how to use it effectively. At

Radio

the end of the course there is an assessment, following which you can obtain an operator's licence.

SSB radio installation is also more complex than VHF, but the good news is that this radio has a far greater range than VHF.

MEDIUM FREQUENCY (MF)

MF has little interest apart from the fact that:

◆ Some coastguard services use it, and keep a listening watch (under the Global Maritime Distress and Safety System – GMDSS).
◆ Ships listen out on it.
◆ There is a calling and distress frequency 2182KHz (rather like Channel 16 on VHF).

MF range depends on the power of transmission. The range of a typical marine radio is up to about 150NM. Higher-power coastal stations are able to push the signal further.

HIGH FREQUENCY (HF)

HF is more useful, but is more of an art. Radio signals in this frequency range are able to reflect off a layer high up in the atmosphere, sometimes multiple times. This means that they can propagate huge distances, sometimes halfway around the world, but in a slightly unpredictable manner. Successful communication to another yacht or to a land-based radio at long range (thousands of miles) is perfectly possible, but depends on:

◆ Radio frequency used
◆ Time of day
◆ Atmospheric conditions, sunspot activity etc (which are largely unpredictable)

There is a choice of frequencies to use, and the frequencies allocated for maritime mobile use are spread throughout the 3–30MHz HF band. The commonly used ones are in the region of 4, 8, 12 and 16MHz.

◆ The lower frequencies work well for 'local' communication (up to a few hundred nautical miles), so a frequency in the 4MHz band will typically be used for yachts staying in touch with each other and for radio 'nets' – a regular communication between a number of participating yachts in a certain area, be they static or crossing an ocean.
◆ Higher frequencies propagate further, and you also get longer-range propagation on all frequencies at nighttime. So if you are contacting Europe from the Caribbean, for example, you might use 12MHz during the day and 8MHz at night.

✳ Tip
Usefully, if you can hear them, they can generally hear you – so once you have found a suitable frequency it will work in both directions.

Communication over a few hundred miles is generally straightforward and reliable, but over longer ranges you may have to try different frequency bands to get a decent signal. So why not use high frequencies all the time, for maximum range? Because:

◆ You are more likely to get more interference from distant radio transmissions.
◆ Higher frequencies, while travelling further, can 'skip' over receivers that are closer to you (because they propagate over long distance by reflecting off the upper atmosphere).

SSB USES

Principal uses of SSB

- ◆ Yacht-to-yacht communication, and radio nets: the ideal way to 'meet' and stay in touch with other yachts on your travels
- ◆ Communication with amateur radio operators at home
- ◆ Participate in amateur weather and routing services
- ◆ Receive weather forecast charts (weather faxes – see page 142)
- ◆ Receive time signals
- ◆ Obtain emergency medical advice from coast radio stations
- ◆ Ship-to-shore telephone calls via coast radio stations, including calls from shore telephone to the yacht, if you monitor a station's 'traffic lists'.

All of the above are free, except for the last one. You need to subscribe to an 'accounting authority' in order to pay for telephone calls made through coast radio stations.

It is also possible to use SSB to link up to internet-type services. To do this, you need:

- ◆ A special modem (PACTOR or equivalent)
- ◆ Connection to a laptop, and suitable software
- ◆ A service provider

Data speeds are slow, and this set-up is aimed at emails etc rather than large files or photos.

The Admiralty List of Radio Signals, which is published in several volumes by the UK Hydrographic office, gives details – particularly frequencies – of coast radio stations, weather services and time signals.

Satellite communication

From mid ocean, the only alternative to radio is line-of-sight communication to satellite, using UHF and higher frequency bands. This is a much more sophisticated communication solution that relies on expensive infrastructure; so, naturally, it is expensive to use. The services available are similar to home:

◆ Telephone
◆ SMS messages
◆ Emails
◆ Internet access

In addition, you can get:

◆ Yacht tracking
◆ Access to assistance and rescue services

✳ Tip
Note that satellite technology develops quite quickly, so it is worth doing your own research to find the most up-to-date solutions.

What you don't get through this medium is the ability to talk to 'anybody out there', which radio gives you. You simply get one-to-one communication, by telephone number (or via the internet).

✳ Tip
As a general rule, the more you pay (for equipment and on-going service) the more you get (data speeds etc).

Satellite communication

Satellite telephone

The simplest option is a hand-held satellite telephone. This gives:

◆ Ordinary telephone communication (at a high cost per minute)
◆ Slow data transfer, through a built-in modem that can be connected to a laptop computer

Telephones can be bought outright, and usage can be pre-paid, or by monthly contract – similar to a mobile phone. There are a number of satellite telephone systems, operated by different providers.

◆ At the time of writing, Iridium seems to be the favourite: it provides total earth coverage via 66 low earth orbit satellites.
◆ Inmarsat achieves coverage everywhere except near the poles, using geostationary satellites. Because the satellites are in a higher orbit there is a perceptible delay for the signal to travel up and back to the earth station (noticeable in a telephone conversation).
◆ Other systems using geostationary satellites (eg Thuraya) cover just part of the world – but depending on where you intend to be, they may be reasonable alternatives. The bad news for sailors is that most of their users tend to be on land, rather than the oceans, so understandably this is where their coverage is focused.

Hand-held telephones need to get a clear view to the satellite in order to operate. Alternatively, you can install a system inside the yacht, connected to an external antenna; this may make it easier to use, particularly if you are connecting to a laptop for data.

Inmarsat C

This is an older satellite system, which is relatively cheap, still serviceable and widely used. It features:

◆ Text-based messages
◆ Short emails (via accounting authority)
◆ Medical/maritime assistance
◆ Weather forecasts (see page 143)
◆ Tracking facility
◆ Distress alerting

The system is used as part of the GMDSS; so, for example, it links directly to maritime rescue co-ordination centres.

Satellite broadband

Moving upmarket, if you want to make meaningful use of internet services, you are going to have to spend more, both for the initial system, and for the quantity of data you access. These systems need an external domed antenna, but with the low-end systems these antennae are now relatively small and weigh only a couple of kilograms.

Both Iridium and Inmarsat provide systems aimed at leisure users, and include voice (telephone). Coverage is the same as the respective satellite telephones, ie:

◆ Worldwide for Iridium (low earth orbit) satellites
◆ Everywhere except the polar regions for Inmarsat geostationary satellites

Moving up the scale, higher-performance VSAT systems are available from Inmarsat and other suppliers, still using relatively small antennae, stabilised to point towards a geostationary satellite. Their coverage depends on the satellites they use, so check this if you are considering such systems.

☀ Tip
Broadband on a yacht will never quite equal what you are used to at home; and the high-end VSAT installations cost nearly as much as a small yacht. For more affordable solutions, data compression services are available, removing large attachments from emails etc, to increase speed and keep data costs down.

Weather information
If you're planning the communications set-up for a long-distance sailing trip, weather information is probably one of the most important factors. You are looking for a suitable combination of:

◆ Forecast service
◆ Means to receive it

Coastal waters
A number of forecast services are generally available in parts of the world where they are needed. They are available from:

◆ VHF
◆ Public local radio
◆ Navtex

24-hour forecasts are widely available, and if you're lucky, three- or five-day outlooks, which are extremely useful for planning coastal passages.

However, these broadcast media are short range (Navtex up to maybe 200NM from the transmitter) and the forecasts focus on the local area. And although useful, spoken forecasts, or text (ie Navtex or SMS), are fundamentally limited if you want to understand the weather patterns and what's going on.

✳ Tip

It is extremely useful to use a voice recorder so that you can record spoken forecasts and play them back slowly afterwards – more so if they are broadcast in a language you're not fluent in.

If you are close enough to the coast for mobile phone/smartphone coverage, you have more options:

◆ SMS and email messages containing weather information (see page 143)
◆ Internet, with its huge range of weather services and different presentations

SSB radio

For ocean passages, the following are worth considering:

◆ Spoken forecasts from some national shortwave radio stations, such as Radio France Internationale
◆ Weather fax
◆ Amateur or professional weather and routeing advice

Spoken forecasts can be useful (particularly tropical storm warnings) but are limited, as mentioned above.

Weather fax, in the form of synoptic charts (see Fig. 7.2), are invaluable for developing a feel for weather patterns and therefore deciding on your passage plan for the next few days. These services are available from a number of shore stations across the world (the *Admiralty List of Radio Signals* has the details of services and radio frequencies).

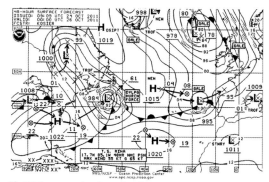

Fig 7.2 An example of weather fax.

To receive them you need:

◆ SSB radio, or the cheaper option of an HF radio receiver
◆ The means to decode and display the faxes, ie a suitable modem
◆ Printer, or laptop with the right software to display the fax

Routeing advice is particularly useful for less experienced ocean sailors. I myself am deeply indebted to Herb Hilgenberg (*Southbound II*) who has now, sadly, ceased his excellent service and sound advice. There are a number of similar individuals who continue to broadcast weather information for vessels on passage.

✳ **Tip**
Skippers receiving any kind of advice from external sources must always remember that the final decision on where to sail is theirs alone. Don't become over-reliant on (or excessively obedient to) distant advice!

Satellite

Clearly, the top-of-the-range solution is broadband internet access, giving a full range of weather services from different forecasters. But more affordable options are available. Inmarsat C can receive weather bulletins in text format, for free. These bulletins are the 'high seas' shipping forecast for whichever metarea you set it. For sailors with 'limited bandwidth', a number of organisations offer to send emails or SMS text messages containing weather information in different formats:

◆ GRIB files: these are coded weather forecasts produced from computer models. With suitable software, they can be displayed as weather charts
◆ Weather forecasts in text
◆ Graphical forecasts: these comprise more data and take longer to receive

This means that even low-end satellite systems (eg satellite phones) can receive useful weather information, but you need to research:

◆ What weather information services are available? Are they sufficient for your needs?
◆ Cost
◆ Ease of use and reliability (eg linking a satellite phone to your laptop)

✳ Tip

In all cases, forecasts are fallible. The longer the range, the less likely they are to be accurate. It is all too easy to 'believe' a precise forecast for 3 to 5 days ahead, but it might be rubbish! Also, bear in mind that GRIB files are produced by computers with no expert intervention by a human forecaster.

Passage planning

Any intended passage is probably part of an overall long-distance route, and one of the key considerations in planning the route is to make the longer passages at a suitable time of year. Assuming that you have planned this (see **Route Planning**, pages 43–51), and your yacht is already suitably equipped (probably months earlier, see **Yacht Preparation**, pages 107–122), this section covers what you need to do immediately before, and during, the passage:

◆ Planning the passage
◆ Preparing the yacht in the days immediately prior to the passage
◆ How you conduct the passage

The passage may be one of the traditional routes, or off the 'beaten track', a distinct route of your own. Either way, many of the same considerations apply, because even with the former (and even with an established rally) you will be very much on your own at sea.

Unless you are very experienced, it's a good idea to gather as much information about the passage as you can – from pilot charts, books such as *World Cruising Routes*, accounts of other sailors' experiences and talking to people. Essentially you need to decide the approximate track you are going to follow, taking into account the great circle route, favourable winds and currents, and any areas of difficulty or potential danger – be they icebergs or shipping lanes.

Note any reasonable alternative destinations. For example, in the North Atlantic how close to the Azores/ Cape Verde Islands/Bermuda does your planned track take you? You could divert to these locations in case of difficulties such as:

◆ A serious problem with the boat
◆ Medical problems
◆ Running out of food or water

It is wise to carry pilotage information and large-scale charts for some of the alternative destinations. This is similar to the coastal 'port of refuge' concept, but you can't just suddenly decide to put in if there's a bit of bad weather; it may take you several days to sail there.

Having decided on the track, the main thing you need to work out is: what is my likely time at sea? This can be calculated knowing the overall distance, roughly how many nautical miles you sail per day in reasonable conditions, and by making allowances for possible adverse winds or calms. You should arrive at a best guess time and a 'worst case'.

Calculating time at sea: example
The Canary Islands–Barbados trade wind route, about 2,800NM, might take 21 or 22 days in a 34ft yacht averaging 130NM per day, but this could easily go over by 6 or 7 days, or perhaps even 10, if you hit funny weather, so 'worst case' might be 32 days.

Apart from time at sea, you make a note of what kind of conditions you are likely to encounter. This will be used to ensure that the yacht is prepared/equipped appropriately.

Preparation
Most of the preparation at this stage is stocking the yacht for the extended time at sea.

✳ Tip
Long-distance yachts are forever repairing, replacing and maintaining gear and systems on board. It's sensible to spend some time working on the 'problems list' before setting off on a long passage, but you may have to prioritise the important items against less important ones and jobs that can be done at sea.

Water
The 'rule of thumb' for water is: a gallon of water per person per day, which covers cooking, drinking and minimal hygiene (eg teeth and rinsing off salt). Other activities like washing up, and a good deal of bodily washing, can be done with sea water. Inexperienced crew will need to be made aware of the importance of water economy and avoiding wastage.

◆ Water usage can be reduced if you carry plenty of bottled drinks, which are a pleasant luxury at sea.
◆ When filling water containers, leave a bit of air so that they float in the sea in an emergency. You can easily monitor the water usage if it is in containers, and if one of them splits you don't lose too much of your reserve.
◆ When calculating the water to be taken on a long passage, allow for at least 50% extra time at sea in case of calms, adverse weather or problems with the boat.

◆ Give some thought to where you stow the water containers on the yacht. They will amount to a considerable weight, so place them low down (for stability) and central (for yacht trim) if at all possible.

◆ Many experienced yachtsmen equip themselves for catching rain, although it would be somewhat harrowing to rely on this. Remember that the initial run-off, from a sail or part of the deck, can be quite salty.

Using a water maker

◆ Make sure you keep it maintained: if you're not using it for a while, the membrane needs to be treated to prevent biological growth and contamination.

◆ Put the water it produces into a smaller container and taste it before adding it to the main tank (any leaks or damage to the membrane can allow salt water into the product).

◆ Keep a reserve so that if it fails you can complete the trip safely (albeit with tighter control over water usage).

Food

Planning for food clearly relates to the expected time at sea and the number of people eating it, but as with water allow for extra time at sea.

If you plan to use refrigeration to preserve your food, you need to have plenty of contingency for generating power and operating fridges/freezers (see page 115).

If you're not planning to rely on refrigeration, you need to give some thought to stocking up with food

Preparation

✳ Tip

Many long-distance sailors carry a considerable stock of tins brought from home and intended as supplies for the overall trip. These can be used in an emergency.

that won't go off, or at least won't do so quickly, in anticipated conditions (hot if you're in the trade winds). Part of the fun of long-distance sailing is figuring this out and getting ideas from fellow sailors.

◆ Many fruits and vegetables will keep for a limited period, so eat them first before falling back on tinned and dried supplies.

◆ Meat can be vacuum-packed in strong plastic to extend its shelf life.

◆ In hot climates long-life milk goes off quickly once opened, so for teas and coffees you may be better off with powdered milk. Similarly, butter becomes irrelevant unless you have a refrigerator.

◆ Learn to bake bread. Fresh bread is easy to make and absolutely delicious. Flour keeps for ages, and sachets of dried yeast work well. It's easy to mix and knead in a large plastic bowl, and the dough rises well in tropical temperatures.

◆ Large pelagic fish can be caught in the open ocean, and these are a delicious source of fresh food. Gear is simple: a very large hook, with an imitation squid 'skirt' on a wire trace, towed with strong nylon, splashing on the surface about 30m behind the boat as you sail along.

◆ If you are storing tins somewhere fairly damp on the boat to save space, make sure the labels don't come off! Or mark them in case they do.

◆ Staples of rice and dried pasta work well. Potatoes keep surprisingly well, too. Dried pulses need to be fully rehydrated by a lot of soaking. Beansprouts are a possibility for fresh green food, or you could grow cress.

◆ Cheese, eggs, nuts, baked beans etc are good sources of protein. Tinned corned beef and tuna are useful and versatile.

✳ Tip

Like the redoubtable Joshua Slocum, in tropical waters you have a fair chance of breakfasting on flying fish that have landed on the deck during the night.

Gas

Most yachts cook with gas, and it's important to carry an adequate supply. Gas bottles can be filled, but you need to be careful. It's not unknown for small amounts of gas to be put into a bottle by crude methods, and for the gas to run out after a couple of days (interestingly, fills of this nature are rarely any cheaper than proper ones). Bottles might also be over-filled. In this case you are not being cheated, but you are being placed in grave danger from gas leaks and explosions.

◆ Try to use gas bottles that are available locally, and used locally, from reputable dealers. You may need to carry or purchase regulators for different bottle types (easy to change on the rubber gas hose with a jubilee clip).

◆ Consider carrying a larger 'domestic' bottle instead of small 'camping' bottles. The former are more widely used in remote locations.

On passage

◆ If you do get fills, weigh the bottle before and after to find out how much you were given.

> Always store gas where any leakage can drain overboard:
>
> ◆ On deck (try to protect bottles from rusting)
> ◆ In a gas locker with overboard drainage
>
> Spills from spare bottles are less likely if the cap is kept on tightly.

On passage

Having decided on a planned track, sailing it is much the same as any coastal passage.

◆ You are likely to be busiest when close to land – look out for fishing boats, shipping etc. In the open sea you are less likely to encounter other vessels.
◆ You don't have to be particularly precise with your course in open sea. Wind vane self-steering comes into its own; you can tolerate the heading varying by perhaps five or ten degrees for a few hours, provided the yacht is sailing well (just keep a note of the average heading in the log).

Using the motor

Most sailing yachts have a restricted supply of fuel available for motoring: perhaps 24–48 hours or so. You can't motor 'out of trouble' to your destination, as you might on a coastal passage; instead you need to have a strategy for how (or if) you plan to use the engine.

The purists don't motor at all (Bernard Moitessier used to remove the propeller before a long passage to give him extra speed). Most of us are more pragmatic than that, but you need to use fuel strategically, eg for:

◆ Getting out to sea, and in at the far end
◆ Getting out of the way of a nasty thunderstorm if there's no wind
◆ Collision avoidance, or other emergencies
◆ Generating electricity (but see page 114)
◆ In a calm, motoring 12 hours or so to a waypoint where you expect favourable wind, eg if you get radio advice of this

Navigation routine

What follows is 'reasonable good practice', based on personal experience. Individual skippers should think it through and decide what is necessary for their own circumstances. The most important principle is to be adequately prepared so that if the GPS or chart plotter goes wrong, you could still navigate with compass and log. The simplest solution is pencil and paper.

LOG KEEPING

A written log is essential for long passages, and makes a great record of the trip. As a minimum, columns should include:

◆ Time (UT or local, with note of time zone)
◆ Log reading
◆ Distance run
◆ Magnetic heading steered (leave a little space after this in case you need to work out the course over ground)
◆ Actual wind speed and direction
◆ GPS fix, latitude and longitude

On passage

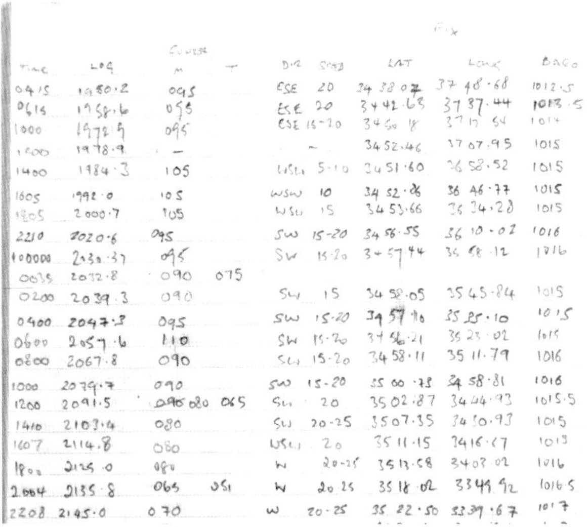

Time	Log	Course M	T	Dir	Speed	Lat	Long	Baro
0415	1950·2	095		ESE	20	34 38 07	37 48·68	1012·5
0615	1958·6	095		ESE	20	34 42·63	37 37·44	1013·5
1000	1972·9	095		ESE	15-20	34 50 18	37 17 54	1014
1200	1978·9	—		—		34 52·46	37 07·95	1015
1400	1984·3	105		WSW	5-10	34 51·60	36 58·52	1015
1605	1992·0	105		WSW	10	34 52·86	36 46·77	1015
1805	2000·7	105		WSW	15	34 53·66	36 34·28	1015
2210	2020·6	095		SW	15-20	34 56·55	36 10·02	1016
000000	2030·37	095		SW	15-20	34 57·44	36 58·12	1016
0035	2032·8	090	075					
0200	2039·3	090		SW	15	34 58·05	35 45·84	1015
0400	2047·3	095		SW	15-20	34 57·10	35 35·10	1015
0600	2057·6	110		SW	15-20	34 56·21	35 23·02	1015
0800	2067·8	090		SW	15-20	34 58·11	35 11·79	1016
1000	2079·7	090		SW	15-20	35 00·73	34 58·81	1016
1200	2091·5	~~090~~ 080	065	SW	20	35 02·87	34 44·93	1015·5
1410	2103·4	080		SW	20-25	35 07·35	34 30·93	1015
1607	2114·8	080		WSW	20	35 11·15	34 16·67	1013
1800	2125·0	080		W	20-25	35 13·58	34 07·02	1016
2004	2135·8	065	051	W	20-25	35 18·02	33 49·92	1016·5
2208	2145·0	070		W	20-25	35 22·50	33 39·67	1017

Fig 8.1 Typical log-book.

- ◆ Barometer (if you are on the alert for tropical storms, also add corrections for diurnal variation)
- ◆ 'Notes', which can be used for a variety of purposes: notes of radio conversations or messages, sightings of land or vessels, distance to waypoint, how slow/fast your chronometer is, absolutely anything of interest

Routine log entries can be made every hour, or two hours, or at change of watch, and whenever you change course. Ad hoc entries can be made any time you want or need to note something: an important radio message, for example, or a gale warning. Yachts on passage normally use an exact mid-day log entry to work out the '24-hour distance run', which is a good measure of progress.

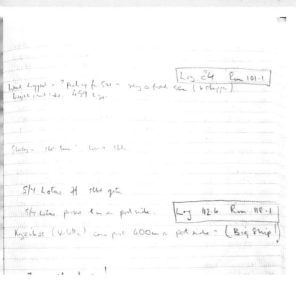

✳ Tip

Always make a log entry for GPS fixes plotted on the chart, because this cuts out a very frequent source of error – misreading the latitude/longitude from the screen while doing the plot.

PAPER CHARTS AND MAGNETIC VARIATION

Even if you use a chart plotter, it's a good idea to carry a paper chart to your destination. It can be quite small-scale because you don't need much charted detail away from land. This chart will also give you magnetic variation. You can mark your GPS position fixes and astro navigation position lines on the chart (label them with date and time) and it will make a good record of your voyage.

On passage

OCEAN CURRENTS

It's important to carry information on ocean currents in order to have any chance of working up an estimated position from course steered and distance run. This information can also inform your choice of course and route. The best way to carry this information is on paper: pilot charts (see page 45). If you download these to your laptop, print a copy.

✳ Tip

You do not need to worry about tides for this, because tidal streams (which are not big off-shore anyway) will average out over 12 hours.

ACCURATE TIME

Maintain one accurate time reference, in case you need to use it for astro navigation. This can be an ordinary electronic watch, capable of keeping time to a few seconds a day. It can be any time zone, as long as you have a note of this. Check it regularly (say, once a day) against the GPS time, and note in the log how many seconds slow or fast it is.

Radio is an alternative source of time signals. There are a number of services that can be received on SSB radio or other MF/HF receiver.

As well as your accurate time reference, keep one clock or watch set to UT, to avoid any confusion when

✳ Tip

Beware of radio time signals that are received via digital radio or, worse, the internet. These are several seconds slow.

using almanacs, the *Admiralty List of Radio Signals* or other UT time references.

ASTRO SIGHTS

There's generally little to do on an ocean sailing passage (unless the weather is bad) so a good use of time is to take some astro sights. This will give you practice and confidence. If astro is to be a viable fall-back in the event of GPS malfunction, you need to prove to yourself that you can do it. If you practise, and compare the results to your GPS fix, you will get better and quicker at it and gain confidence in the results.

> ✳ **Tip**
>
> At twilight, or if you can see the horizon in bright moonlight, have a go at the planets and stars. If you get a ridiculous result, it may be because you identified the body incorrectly. Don't throw away the sight: just rework the sight reduction once you've worked out which star or planet it is.

Everyone can have a go, and if the resulting position line puts you in the wrong ocean, a more experienced navigator can go through the form and spot the mistake. Once the calculation is re-worked you can confirm the quality of the original site.

> ✳ **Tip**
>
> Note that if you do lose the GPS, and have to revert to estimated positions and astro position fixes, you may need to revise your plans for landfall. Pick something you are likely to see, rather than a small low island.

On passage

COMPASS AND LOG CHECKS

With GPS, assuming you're reasonably happy that the fixes are progressing in the right direction, you tend not to worry about the accuracy of the compass, let alone the log. But it's good practice to check these things, in case you need to rely on them.

To keep the log monitored, work up dead reckoning and estimated position over a 24-hour period between GPS fixes. Investigate any major or consistent discrepancy. Clean the log impeller, and check it against the GPS over a shorter distance on a consistent course.

For most coastal sailors compass deviation is rarely, if ever, checked. But it does matter if you are sailing for several days in the same direction. To check the compass deviation:

◆ Compare the steering compass with a reading of the heading on the hand-bearing compass.
◆ Check the steering compass against the calculated true heading towards the sun, or other astro body (see page 106).

Crew routine

Skipper and crew are central to the whole enterprise. They need to function well as a team, and managing this, together with crew welfare, is probably the skipper's most important task. Don't underestimate the challenging conditions, particularly in the first few days, as you are getting used to:

◆ An unnatural work/rest routine
◆ Living in a small space at sea
◆ The constant motion of a small yacht

WATCHES

The purpose of a watch system is to organise the crew to carry out essential tasks, while at the same time ensuring that everyone gets enough rest. Generally, the 'on watch' crew is responsible for keeping the yacht sailing.

On a small yacht with, say, three people, it's quite reasonable (assuming that you have self-steering) for a single crew member to be on watch on their own. Their job is to 'babysit' the boat:

◆ Keep an eye on sail trim, and course being steered.
◆ Watch for changing wind strength or signs of it (eg approaching squalls).
◆ Keep a lookout.

If a sail change or reef is needed they can call someone else for assistance; but on an average watch they can spend much of their time reading, drinking cups of tea or fishing. The advantage is that everyone gets plenty of off watch time during which they can sleep, relax and do the domestic tasks such as food preparation.

✴ Tip

It's important to have rules about wearing a harness and clipping on, if you're on solo watch – particularly at night.

With a larger crew you can have a 'team' on watch, and perhaps more formality about who is responsible for domestic tasks. You can still give everyone plenty of off watch time.

On passage

Other sailing/navigation tasks that the skipper may look after themselves or delegate to the watch team are:

◆ Log entries
◆ Navigation checks/decisions
◆ Radio schedules and weather forecasts
◆ Routine checks and maintenance
◆ Power-generating routine and monitoring

✳ Tip
Some skippers/crews prefer distinct day/night watch periods, eg six-hour watches during the day, three hours at night. I prefer to keep it as simple as possible and have one system running for 24 hours, e.g. for a crew of three, two hours on and four hours off.

DOMESTIC TASKS AND CREW WELLBEING
With a small crew, the tasks of food preparation and washing up are small; they tend to be organised fairly informally, eg someone who feels hungry after their sleep will volunteer to cook.

✳ Tip
Some yachts have a 'happy hour' with one beer a day. This may be good for crew morale, but be aware that with any alcohol you will need more sleep, which is a poor idea if you are already tired. Most crews seem to make up for this when they reach land ...

A larger crew needs more planning and organisation. Preparing a meal for eight people, and clearing up afterwards, are non-trivial tasks; the work needs to be shared fairly, and meals need to be organised so that individuals asleep after their watch don't miss out. So it's a good idea to have a daily mealtime plan and duty rota to fit in with the watch system.

✳ Tip
Establish a routine for rubbish disposal. At sea, anything biodegradable can be thrown overboard – other material is compacted (tins crushed etc), bagged and stored for disposal on arrival.

'Ship's time', for meals and watches, can be the time zone you're currently in, or you can keep to the zone you departed from.

- Try to have at least one time during the day when the whole crew can be together for a meal; this is good for crew morale.
- Make sure everyone is getting enough rest and sleep.
- Take care with food hygiene when preparing food. Antibacterial soap is useful in the galley.
- Washing up can be done in sea water to conserve the fresh water supply, but don't neglect hygiene.
- Make sure that everyone is eating enough, and drinking enough water. Individual bottles can help to share water out if it is tight, and can also show if individuals are drinking enough.
- If you use salt water for washing, make sure you clean the salt off to prevent skin sores. Baby wipes can be useful (but mustn't be put in the heads).

On passage

◆ Make sure the crew have enough protective clothing, be it waterproofs and thermals or sunhats and sunglasses.
◆ Protect yourself from the sun with hats, glasses, lightweight long-sleeved shirts and sun cream.
◆ Protect your feet by wearing deck shoes or decent sandals.

The main principle on a yacht at sea is to support each other. Be aware if someone is finding the conditions difficult, and help them through it.

✳ Tip
Once you have been at sea for a few days you will probably be more used to the conditions and the routine, and have plenty of time on your hands. Make sure you bring enough books to read and share.

The risk of problems occurring while sailing in the open ocean is not much greater than coastal sailing. But it's vital to realise that if anything does go wrong you are considerably further away from assistance. To a large extent you need to be prepared to deal with it yourself – or survive for a considerable time before rescue.

This section looks at some of the things that could go wrong with your yacht or crew on an ocean passage. The focus is:

◆ Prevention, by being very aware of the dangers and consequences
◆ Preparation, in terms of training and equipment carried on board
◆ What to do in emergency situations

> With the greater accessibility of ocean sailing to ordinary people, and many trouble-free passages, the assumption inevitably grows that ocean sailing is safe, or even easy. Never lose sight of the enormity of crossing an ocean, or the considerable achievement of preparing and looking after a small yacht and crew during the passage. Incidents may be few, but the consequences are on a different scale to any other type of sailing.

Medical/accident

Unless you are a doctor, this is the area where you are probably least prepared. The concept of first aid – keeping a casualty going for the 30 minutes or so that it takes the ambulance to arrive – is out. Instead you will have to deal with problems that arise at sea, and to do this it makes sense to carry some equipment and medicines.

Medical/accident

Information and training

If you're new to this, there are courses available, for example the one-day RYA First Aid at Sea and the more comprehensive five-day Medical Care at Sea. It's helpful to carry a good first-aid manual, and reference books such as *The Ship Captain's Medical Guide*.

You also need a plan to get medical advice at sea, in an emergency. This can be:

◆ SSB radio, via coast radio station
◆ SSB radio via radio net. There are plenty of doctors who are long-distance sailors, and this can be the best way to get advice, and even assistance at sea
◆ Satellite telephone
◆ Satellite text services such as Inmarsat C

Prevention of accidents

In view of the consequences, your crew need to be particularly aware of the dangers of accidents. The best thing is to give everyone a safety briefing at the start of the trip; and remind them of relatively mundane risks, such as companionway steps or falling out of bed.

Useful precautions

◆ If you're cooking when it's rough, wear water-proofs in case you spill hot pans/liquids. Half-fill mugs with hot drinks, and place them in the sink while filling them.
◆ Take particular care with knives and fish hooks.
◆ Don't attempt to go up the mast at sea. That lost halyard can wait; use a spare, or the topping lift.
◆ Don't attempt to repair a generator.
◆ Keep the boat tidy.

◆ Close hatches/companionways when working on deck.
◆ No bare feet on deck.
◆ Always use a preventer on the boom.
◆ Teach everyone proper winch use.
◆ Look after yourselves:
  ● Don't get sunburned or cold.
  ● Wash sensitive skin and keep as dry as possible to prevent sores.
  ● Drink plenty of fluids.

Chronic conditions

Anyone with a long-term illness, or condition such as asthma or diabetes, or who is pregnant, should have a careful discussion with their doctor before they embark on the trip. They need to have a good supply of their regular medicines, a good understanding of the condition, and additional treatments in case of any exacerbations.

Equipment and medicines

✳ Tip
'Official' advice, such as the list of medicines required for Category 0 MCA coding, is of limited value. Talk instead to a knowledgeable practitioner, who will probably advise against carrying some of the 'required' medicines.

This is an area where you need to make your own decisions based on your own knowledge, training and assessment of risk; ideally in discussion with a doctor or pharmacist with an understanding of the situation.

Medical/accident

Medicines to consider

◆ First-aid kit (bandages, plasters, adhesive sutures, splints etc)
◆ Seasickness pills
◆ Antiseptic/anaesthetic creams, and nappy rash cream for skin discomfort
◆ Suntan lotion and aftersun moisturiser
◆ Insect repellant
◆ Painkillers (consider different types and strengths)
◆ Antihistamines for allergies
◆ Diarrhoea and constipation remedies
◆ Burn creams, and paraffin gauze and cling film for burns
◆ Antibiotics (and information on how/when to use the different types)
◆ Thermometer
◆ Blood pressure monitor (this can be useful for someone providing radio medical advice)
◆ Adrenaline auto-injector
◆ Oxygen (also useful in any diving accident)
◆ Skin glue, to close small cuts and grazes
◆ Babywipes
◆ Hot water bottle

Other emergency scenarios
Fire and gas

Here the normal precautions apply:

◆ Follow a rigorous gas routine.
◆ Stow a fire blanket by the cooker.
◆ Carry fire extinguishers.
◆ Carry buckets.
◆ Consider a deck wash/fire hose.

◆ If you do need to abandon to the liferaft, you will need to get to the grab bag, EPIRB, food and water supplies; so think about where you stow these.

Flooding/sinking

As with coastal sailing:

◆ Monitor the water in the bilge.
◆ Carry bungs for skin fittings.

In the ocean you won't hit any rocks, but there is a small risk of striking a partially submerged object such as a container. If this happens you will certainly hear it, and emergency action may be necessary:

◆ Stem the flow if possible, with anything available: cushions, sails (possibly from the outside).
◆ Close any bulkhead doors.
◆ Carry a mask and wetsuit so you can inspect the damage.
◆ Prepare to abandon to the liferaft if you have to (see page 170).

Mechanical and rig failure

It's sensible to have the yacht thoroughly checked before departing, and to carry spares and tools to cope with a number of eventualities – see the **Yacht preparation** section on pages 107–122.

Remember to carry rigging shears and/or a 'dedicated' hacksaw to deal with a possible rigging failure in rough weather (you don't want the mast to damage the hull).

If you suffer a serious failure, you may have to use your own ingenuity to devise a jury rig to continue the passage.

Other emergency scenarios

Man overboard

This is a nightmare scenario at the best of times. With ocean sailing the risk is that, with a small crew and perhaps solo watches, someone could go overboard unnoticed. The answer is to have a firm rule about clipping on:

◆ At night
◆ If you are on your own (ie everyone else is below, possibly asleep)

In hot weather it may be preferable to use a simple harness (ie not necessarily one that is built into a lifejacket).

Some solo sailors trail a warp behind the yacht, and others wear electronic alarm devices, but the simplest thing is not to go overboard in the first place, so CLIP ON.

> I had one crew member who didn't want to clip on, because he was prepared to risk his own life. I said I respected that, but didn't want our yacht, and all the other yachts we were in contact with, to have to conduct a futile search for several days; or to have to tell his mother. He clipped on.

Piracy

Piracy attacks at sea are an unfortunate reality, even though the principal targets are larger ships and their cargo. You have to remember that yachts – even old and tatty ones – represent the possibility of huge riches in poor parts of the world so they can be magnets for simple theft. And in some areas, where there is little established law and order, the possibility of ransom is a reality, as some well-publicised stories attest.

Modern pirates are well armed and equipped with fast motorboats, so the possibility of resistance or escape is slim. Calls for help are reliant on the presence of a naval force that is capable of assisting you, and willing to come to your aid.

The advice is:

◆ Avoid parts of the world where it happens. Coastal waters of countries suffering a state of lawlessness or civil war are particularly dangerous.
◆ Get advice before your trip, as part of your route planning.
◆ Keep your ear to the ground by listening to other yachts on SSB radio nets – word spreads fast, particularly where security is concerned.

There are some parts of the world – eg the approach to the southern Red Sea – where yachts want or need to pass, despite the danger. In these cases groups of yachts sometimes form convoys and stick together, perhaps observing radio silence for part of the passage. This can reduce, but not eliminate, the danger of piracy.

Assistance and rescue
Assistance
Surprisingly often, yachts go to each other's assistance when they are aware of a problem (usually via an SSB net). The kind of assistance that fellow yachts can offer, in non-emergency situations, is likely to be far more flexible than a rescue co-ordinated by a national coast guard.

For example, if you suffer a rig failure, or a non-life-threatening medical emergency that you cannot deal with on your own, another yacht may be able to provide the necessary tool, medicine or expertise to allow you to continue on your passage.

Unless it is a clear emergency, this kind of assistance is preferable to an expensive ocean rescue that will probably require you to abandon your yacht and its contents.

Distress signals

The simplest and most immediate method of signalling a Mayday from mid ocean is an Emergency Position Indicating Radio Beacon (EPIRB).

This is a small floating device, self-contained with its own battery (lasting 48 hours), that transmits a distress message direct to satellite on 406MHz. This enables the message to reach a rescue co-ordination centre within 45 minutes. The message contains information that enables the rescue co-ordinating authority to identify the vessel to which the EPIRB is registered.

The basic signal enables the transmitter to be located to within three miles. Devices with built-in GPS transmit their position to 50m or so, updated regularly. Some EPIRBs also transmit on 121.5MHz, a VHF frequency that allows aircraft and search vessels to home in on the beacon.

'Personal' EPIRBs, designed to be worn, are much smaller and have less battery life.

Alternative methods to signal distress

◆ Mayday on VHF Channel 16 – you would be very lucky to be heard on this, as the range to another vessel is only 20–30NM.

◆ Mayday call on MF radio, 2182kHz: range 200NM or so, depending on power and time of day, and the message may be picked up by a ship keeping MF radio watch. Radio silence is kept from 00 to 03, and 30 to 33 minutes past the hour for urgent traffic; this is the best time to be heard.

◆ Inmarsat C distress message.
◆ SART (Search and Rescue Transponder), which produces a distinctive pattern on a scanning radar display. This relies on a ship being close enough to scan you with radar.

Rescue

The most likely scenario for a rescue is:

◆ EPIRB message is received by the maritime rescue co-ordination centre (MRCC) for the ocean area.
◆ MRCC contacts vessels in the area.
◆ Airborne search started if necessary/feasible.
◆ Nearby commercial shipping responds and diverts to the casualty.
◆ Crew rescued by a commercial ship, which continues to its destination.

This is a far cry from coastal rescue/assistance by a lifeboat. Depending on where you are, it can take a significant time for assistance to reach you. Even the 48-hour duration of the EPIRB signal starts to look short in an ocean rescue scenario.

Given that the rescuing vessel is most likely to be a commercial ship diverting from its planned course, neither ship nor crew will be equipped for search and rescue or recovery operations such as investigating wreckage. It is at this stage that a SART would be most useful, because it would make it significantly easier for a ship to locate a small yacht or liferaft.

Survival

Abandoning the yacht and taking to a liferaft is something you do when there is absolutely no alternative.
But if it happens:

◆ You may need to act quickly.
◆ You need to take with you anything that will aid survival and rescue.

✳ Tip
Next time your liferaft is serviced, go and have a
look at it, and check out the emergency equipment
that it carries. It's helpful to know what to expect if
you have to use it.

Yachts generally organise a 'grab bag' containing the
essentials, or at least some of them. Other items can
be grabbed separately, particularly if they are large and
float. Plan and list what to take, pack your waterproof
grab bag, and stow it somewhere accessible even if you
have a fire on board.

Emergency supplies
◆ **Water** Store water in containers, leave some air
   so that they float. In the grab bag: hand-operated reverse osmosis water maker and drinking
   bottle for rationing.
◆ **Food** Take cans, dry food and spear gun. In the
   grab bag: can opener, fishing line, knife and
   board.
◆ **Rescue** Take the EPIRB and flares in a floating
   container. In the grab bag: hand-held VHF, hand-
   held GPS, SART, torch, batteries, heliograph
   (mirror), whistle, waterproof notepad, pencils.

◆ **Care of crew** Wear lifejackets. Take clothing, blankets and thermal protective aids for warmth. In the grab bag: medicines (including seasickness tablets), sun cream, waterproof matches.
◆ **Dinghy** Take this or other craft for additional space.

A one-day Sea Survival Course is highly recommended, because it is very often the first and only opportunity for people to:

◆ See a liferaft inflated.
◆ Go into the water fully clothed and wearing a lifejacket.
◆ Try to get into the liferaft.
◆ Experience what it's like to be in a liferaft, with other people.

If nothing else it will convince you that abandoning to the liferaft is very much a last option; in particular, it would be horrendous in rough conditions. The course also covers the principles of survival.

Key survival principles
◆ Maintain individual and crew morale.
◆ Care for individual crew members.
◆ Maintaining a functioning watch system as on the yacht, to look after your craft, navigate and to keep a lookout for search vessels and aircraft.
◆ Keep a positive attitude to the likelihood of rescue and/or alternative strategies such as landfall.

Glossary

acceleration zone Area of stronger local wind.

AIS (Automatic Identification System) VHF system for sending/receiving information about ships, to aid collision avoidance.

altitude (astro navigation) Angle of a celestial body above the horizon.

anticyclone Area of high pressure, with clockwise wind circulation in the northern hemisphere (anticlockwise in the southern).

assumed position (also assumed latitude, assumed longitude) Position on the earth close to your own position, used in astro navigation to construct a position line.

astronomical (astro) navigation The process of determining your position by measuring the altitude of a celestial body at a precise time.

autopilot Electronic device for steering a yacht.

azimuth (astro navigation) True bearing of a celestial body.

back (of wind) Change direction anticlockwise eg N to NW to W.

celestial body The sun, moon, a planet or star.

chart datum Framework used for representing the latitude and longitude of points on the chart (eg WGS84).

chart projection Method used for representing the curved surface of the earth on the flat plane of a chart.

current Movement of water in the oceans (other than tidal motion).

Coriolis Effect, or force, caused by the rotation of the earth. Effect is caused by using the rotating earth as a 'stationary' frame of reference.

cyclone A tropical revolving storm in the Indian Ocean or South Pacific. 'Extra-tropical cyclone' is a low pressure weather system. 'Cyclonic': the wind directions associated with such a system.

dangerous semicircle The side of a tropical revolving storm that is more dangerous to shipping.

declination Angle of a celestial body north or south of the equator.

doldrums see **ITCZ**

EPIRB (Emergency Position-Indicating Radio Beacon) Self-contained device for signalling distress, via satellite and to aircraft.

equation of time Time difference between 1200 UT/GMT and the sun's meridian passage at Greenwich.

eye (of storm) Small calm area at the centre of a tropical revolving storm.

funnel effect Increased wind as it passes between land features constricting its flow.

geostrophic wind Wind associated with straight isobars.

Galileo European satellite navigation system.

GHA (Greenwich Hour Angle) Angle of a celestial body west of Greenwich meridian.

GLONASS Russian satellite navigation system.

GMDSS (Global Maritime Distress and Safety System) Internationally agreed set of procedures and protocols for maritime safety and rescue.

GMT (Greenwich Mean Time) Time based on the sun at Greenwich meridian.

Gnomonic projection Chart projection on which any great circle is a straight line.

GNSS (Global Navigation Satellite System) Generic name for satellite navigation systems.

GPS (Global Positioning System) US (Military) satellite navigation system.

great circle Circle on a sphere whose centre is the centre of the sphere. Shortest distance between two points on the sphere.

GRIB (Gridded Binary) file Weather information data file.

HF (High Frequency) Radio frequency band 3–30MHz.

horse latitudes Area of sub-tropical high pressure and light winds.

hurricane A tropical revolving storm in the Atlantic ocean.

Inmarsat C Satellite system used for basic text communication. Part of GMDSS.

intercept (astro navigation) Distance between assumed position and own position.

international date line Line between time zones 12 and −12 where the date changes (defined by international agreement).

isobar Line joining points of equal atmospheric pressure.

ITCZ (Intertropical Convergence Zone) Area near the equator, between the trade wind belts, where the wind is light and variable.

katabatic wind Wind caused by cold air flowing down steeply sloping ground.

land breeze Night time breeze from the land, caused by air cooling and subsiding.

latent heat Energy needed to evaporate water – which turns to heat when the water condenses.

LHA (Local Hour Angle) Angle of celestial body west of a local position (eg assumed position).

limb (upper, lower) Edge of sun or moon used for astro sight.

magnetic deviation Error of magnetic compass on a boat, due to nearby magnetic influences.

magnetic variation Difference between true and magnetic north at a particular position.

Mercator projection Chart projection most normally used for navigation, with lines of latitude and longitude forming an orthogonal (right-angle) grid.

meridian passage Event when a celestial body passes the observer's meridian, and is directly north or south of the observer. Local noon (for the sun).

MF (Medium Frequency) Radio frequency band 300kHz–3MHz.

monsoon Seasonal wind in the north Indian ocean/southern Asia.

navigable semicircle The side of a tropical revolving storm that is less dangerous to shipping.

pilot chart Chart containing data of average sea and climate conditions, month by month.

position line Line on a chart drawn so that your position is somewhere on that line.

reverse osmosis Method of purifying water by pumping it at high pressure through a membrane.

rhumb line Course of constant (true) heading: straight line on a Mercator projection chart.

roaring forties Area in the forties south latitudes, notorious for gales.

sea breeze Daytime breeze towards land, caused by heating and convection over the land.

sextant Optical device for measuring the angle between two distant objects.

sight reduction Process of working out the intercept and azimuth from an astro observation.

SSB Single Side Band Radio technology which transmits/receives only a single frequency modulated part of the radio signal (upper or lower side band) and not the carrier frequency.

standard time Time (generally a number of hours before or after UT) adopted by a country or region as their 'official' time.

temperate zone Area of the world between the tropics and the polar regions, from about 30° to 60° north and south.

time zone Area of the world that adopts a single standard time – generally spanning about 15° of latitude.

tornado Violent rotating wind vortex, typically a few hundred metres across, that develops mainly over land in hot weather.

trade wind Steady winds from the north-east or south-east that are typical around 10° to 20° north and south.

tropical revolving storm Intensely violent weather system which develops over the sea during the hottest season in the tropics. Also called a tropical cyclone, hurricane, typhoon or cyclone.

typhoon A tropical revolving storm in the north Pacific ocean.

UT (Universal Time) The world-wide reference time (based on GMT).

veer (of wind) Change direction clockwise eg W to NW to N.

VHF (Very High Frequency) Radio frequency band 30–300MHz.

VSAT (Very Small Aperture Terminal) High-end satellite communication technology.

waterspout Tornado over water which develops a column of spray raised by the wind.

wind vane Mechanical device that steers the yacht at a constant set angle to the wind.